AF608083

THE DIVISION OF PARISHES

A Historical Synopsis and a Commentary

THE CATHOLIC UNIVERSITY OF AMERICA
CANON LAW STUDIES
No. 281

The Division of Parishes

A Historical Synopsis and a Commentary

BY

REVEREND EDWARD P. McCASLIN, M.A., S.T.L., J.C.L.
PRIEST OF THE ARCHDIOCESE OF OMAHA

A DISSERTATION

SUBMITTED TO THE FACULTY OF THE SCHOOL OF CANON LAW OF THE CATHOLIC UNIVERSITY OF AMERICA IN PARTIAL FULFILLMENT OF THE REQUIREMENTS FOR THE DEGREE OF DOCTOR OF CANON LAW

THE CATHOLIC UNIVERSITY OF AMERICA PRESS
WASHINGTON, D. C.
1951

NIHIL OBSTAT:

EDUARDUS G. ROELKER, S.T.D., J.C.D.

Washingtonii, D. C., die 16 Aprilis, 1948

IMPRIMATUR:

GERALDUS T. BERGAN, D.D.

Archiepiscopus Omahensis

Omahae, die 19 Aprilis, 1948

MURRAY & HEISTER
WASHINGTON, D. C.

PRINTED BY
TIMES AND NEWS PUBLISHING CO.
GETTYSBURG, PA., U.S.A.

DEDICATED
To My
BELOVED PARENTS

TABLE OF CONTENTS

TABLE OF CONTENTS (Continued)

FOREWORD

The parish unit has been the chief means by which the Church has reached the souls she has been divinely commissioned to teach and guide. History is replete with evidence of her concern for the parochial institute, with proof of her constant efforts to improve and enlarge the opportunities of her subjects to come to a better knowledge of the truths of faith through the betterment of the parishes with which they are affiliated.

Since parishes have as their *raison d'etre* the spiritual welfare of human souls, it is only natural that their nature and existence should be flexible enough to meet the needs of everyone. Men will move from place to place, and environment will sometimes force a dislocation of people in a whole nation or in a small locality. Very early in the life of the Church it can be seen that, while stability of institutions was most desirable, and while there was a genuine reluctance to disturb the status of parishes, yet, when division or some other form of modification was necessary to carry on effective care of souls, the Church was quick to act. Changes in status, and the legislation governing those changes, are found as early as the eighth century. Various modifications could occur, according to the need and the most effective means of supplying it. Union of one parish with another, dismemberment, or the concession of a portion of one parish to another already existing, suppression, or complete division could be necessary, and there was legislation governing each form of adjustment. It is with the division of parishes that this dissertation is concerned.

An understanding of the present law concerning the division of parishes requires a knowledge of the earlier law, particularly in view of the fact that it is from the latter that the various concepts concerning the nature of division, the causes which warrant it in a given case, the allocation of an endowment, and the authorities to whom the law concedes the power to effect the division have their beginning and present signification. Consequently, a historical study of early legislation regarding the division of parishes, followed by a synopsis of the law as presented by the Council of Trent and later regulations issuing from the Holy See, is presented.

The second part of this work interprets the present law of the Code, treating singly the various formalities which the law outlines when a division is undertaken. A brief discussion concerning the application of the law to religious, national, and Oriental parishes completes the work.

The author wishes to acknowledge his profound gratitude to the late Archbishop of Omaha, His Excellency, the Most Reverend James Hugh Ryan, for the opportunity to pursue advanced studies. He is also most grateful to all others who have assisted him in this work by their guidance and direction, particularly the Faculty of the School of Canon Law of The Catholic University of America.

PART ONE

Historical Synopsis

CHAPTER I

The Division of Parishes Before the Council of Trent

ARTICLE 1. FUNDAMENTAL NOTIONS

The specific purpose of this work is to discover the original legislation of the Church governing the division of parishes, to trace its development through history, and to analyze the present law of the Church as it is found in the Code.[1] Prior to any perusal of the steps in the development of the present law, and preparatory to any analysis of the regulations that affect the division of parishes today, it is advisable to establish some preliminary fundamental notions which will find application throughout the work.

Some general notions concerning the various changes of status which can be wrought in parochial benefices must be thoroughly understood for a complete grasp of the thought and the terminology, presented both in the earlier legislation and in the law of the Code itself.

Authors treated of the possible modifications or changes in status under the title of *innovation*.[2] A modification was "any alteration in the benefice which affects the condition in which it was when originally erected."[3] More fully defined, it was the change of the original status of some ecclesiastical office as regards spiritual rights, temporal rights, obligation, location, field of endeavor, or type.[4]

---

[1] *Codex Iuris Canonici Pii X Pontificis Maximi iussu digestus Benedicti Papae XV Auctoritate promulgatus, Praefatione, Fontium annotatione et Indice Analytico-Alphabetico ab Emo Petro Card. Gasparri Auctus* (Romae: Typis Polyglottis Vaticanis, 1917) canons 1427 and 1428.

[2] Wernz (1842-1914), *Jus Decretalium* (3. ed., 6 vols., Prati, 1913-1914), II, 254.

[3] Mundy, *The Union of Parishes,* The Catholic University of America Canon Law Studies, n. 204 (Washington, D. C.: The Catholic University of America Press, 1945), p. 2.

[4] Wernz, *Jus Decretalium,* II, n. 254.

Certain general conditions were demanded in the pre-Code law before a parish could be modified in any way. This was logical, since a change of any kind in benefices was considered a *res odiosa.*[5] Inasmuch as a modification of parishes was permitted only for very grave reasons,[6] it could be accomplished only by a legitimate superior who, alone or together with others, had determined the sufficiency of the causes which were urged as reasons for change.[7] Furthermore, the change of status of a parochial benefice was not to prove harmful in any way to the rights of a third person; for example, a person who had endowed a church with certain stipulations agreed to by the proper ecclesiastical authorities could have prevented the change if he so desired, if there was any danger to the rights guaranteed him at the time he became patron.[8] Again, before modification all interested parties were to be heard by the bishop. These were the pastor, who was always to be consulted, or the parishioners, whose opinions concerning the projected change were to be sought on the grounds that the change would affect them primarily.[9]

These general conditions were demanded in the case of all types of minor benefices subject to the jurisdiction of the bishop. More particularly, they were considered essential to the process of the modification of all parishes. The status of the parochial benefice could be changed in several ways: by union with another, by a change of site, by division, dismemberment, transmutation, or suppression. The present Code, as will be seen later, defines the meaning of these terms, and follows the older concepts and legal requisites very closely.[10] Historically these changes of status grew out

---

[5] Council of Tours (1163)—c. 8, X, *de praebendis et dignitatibus,* III, 5.

[6] Cf. Conc. Trident., sess. XXI, *de ref.,* c. 5.

[7] Wernz, *op. cit., loc. cit.;* Schmalgrueber (1663-1735), *Jus Ecclesiasticum Universum* (5 vols. in 12, Romae, 1843-1845), Lib. III, tit. 48, nn. 10-11 (hereafter cited Schmalgrueber).

[8] Conc. Trident., sess. XXI, *de ref.,* c. 4; cf. S.R.R., *Sedunen.,* 2 apr. 1912—*Sacrae Romanae Rotae Decisiones seu Sentententiae quae . . . prodierunt anno 1909-1939* (31 vols., Romae: Typis Vaticanis, 1912-1948), IV (1912), 153, n. 5 (hereafter cited *Decisiones*).

[9] C. 3, X, *de ecclesiis aedificandis vel reparandis,* III, 48.

[10] Canons 1419 and 1421.

of the need of the Church to accommodate herself to changing conditions in given localities, to the fluctuation of population, to the increase or decrease of wealth, and to the varying opportunities for more effective care of souls. Although change was looked upon with reluctance[11] these reasons often demanded a change of one type or another. Behind the reluctance to alter a parochial benefice was the ancient concept that those responsible for the erection of a parish could be considered as parties to a tacit contract whereby mutual rights and obligations were decided upon. Hence, any change in the original contract was held to be a kind of breach, and one party to the contract to be deprived of a claim.[12] Such an attitude, however, was not as inflexible as might appear, since on occasion there was legislation which made change compulsory.[13]

With these basic concepts of modification in general to serve as a kind of guide, the detailed treatment of the legislation concerning division will be found to coincide in particular cases with the general principles outlined above.

ARTICLE 2. LEGISLATION CONCERNING DIVISION BEFORE THE COUNCIL OF TRENT

Commentators on the Decretal law defined the division of parishes as the constitution of two or more parishes from one in such a way that, where formerly there had been one parish, now two or more existed.[14] They insisted that such a division was not the ordinary thing, but that the requirements of law had to be strictly adhered to, and for reasons that will be considered in the next chapter.

---

[11] Conc. Trident., sess. XXIV, *de ref.*, c. 5; Mundy, *The Union of Parishes*, p. 17.

[12] Laurentius (1861-1927), *Institutiones Juris Canonici* (Friburgi Brisgoviae, 1903), n. 236.

[13] Conc. Trident., sess. XXI, *de ref.*, c. 4; c. 4, C. XVI, q. 1—Jaffé (1819-1870), *Regesta Pontificum Romanorum ab condita Ecclesia ad annum post Christum natum MCXCVIII* (2. ed., correctam et auctam auspiciis Gulielmi Wattenbach curaverunt S. Loewenfeld, F. Kaltenbrunner, P. Ewald, 2 vols. in 1. Lipsiae, 1885-1888), n. 1202 (hereafter cited Jaffé).

[14] Schmalzgrueber, Lib. V, tit. 5, n. 204; Reiffenstuel (1642-1703), Jus Ecclesiasticum Universum (5 vols. in 7, Parisiis, 1864-1870), Lib. III, tit. 12, n. 21 (hereafter cited Reiffenstuel).

Since parishes were considered as minor benefices in the Decretal law, and as such were very often designated by the term *praebendae,*[15] it is necessary to investigate the difference between these minor benefices and the so-called major ones. Briefly, the chief distinction was this, that those who possessed major benefices had ordinary jurisdiction in the external forum. Sometimes the term was also applied to persons enjoying some primacy of honor, such as certain members of the Roman Curia.[16] Examples of those who possessed ordinary jurisdiction in the external forum were the bishops, the prelates *nullius,* and certain other superior prelates.[17]

Minor benefices were those whose incumbents were without that special preeminence of honor and ordinary jurisdiction. Among these was the benefice of pastor.[18] It is sufficient for the purpose of this work to determine that when the law spoke of the division of parishes it referred to them as minor benefices. Often the principles which were applied to the division of parishes were derived from those that were used in the division of minor benefices.[19]

As the development of parishes in Europe and in the British Isles flourished, especially during the period of the proprietary churches, it became necessary that some procedure be drawn up for safeguarding the rights of parishes and pastors from which territory and people were taken. It was only logical that rights could have been subject to much abuse had bishops been allowed to remove sections of territory and groups of parishioners from the old parishes simply out of caprice or for reasons without much foundation in law. Since the payment of tithes and other fees had become a matter of serious obligation,[20] and inasmuch as Charle-

---

[15] Cf. e.g., c. 8, X, *de praebendis et dignitatibus,* V, III; c. 2, C. 1, q. 3.

[16] Wernz, *Jus Decretalium,* II, n. 254.

[17] Wernz, *op. cit., loc. cit.;* c. 2, X, *de iudiciis,* II, 1.

[18] C. 4, X, *de clerico aegrotante,* III, 6.

[19] An example of such a principle is found in the Council of Mainz (813), c. 41—Mansi (1692-1769), *Sacrorum Conciliorum Nova et Amplissima Collectio* (53 vols. in 60, Parisiis, 1901-1927), XVI, 74. Cf. c. 24, C. XVI, q. 3.

[20] II Council of Mâcon (585), c. 5: "Unde statuimus . . . ut mos antiquus a fidelibus reparetur. . . . Quas leges Christianorum congeries longis temporibus custodivit intemeratas."—Mansi, IX, 952; Kremer, *Church Support in the United States,* The Catholic University of America Canon Law Studies, n. 61 (Washington, D. C.: The Catholic University of America, 1930), p. 11.

magne (768-814) in his determination to indemnify the Church for the secularizations which had occurred earlier, had in 779 enforced the traditional regulations regarding the payment of tithes in the Frankish kingdom,[21] such regulations became even more necessary. Most of the legislation during Carolingian times gives evidence of the meticulous care with which the rights of the mother church were protected when a division became necessary.[22] From this legislation it can be determined that any division was viewed with disfavor. A council of Mainz (813) made it clear that the mother church was always to be protected.[23]

Most of the earlier legislation tended to support the right of the mother church to a constant claim on the income growing out of the tithes, stole fees, and other sources of revenue, as well as on the continued presence at all services of the faithful who belonged to the parish. Out of this situation there developed legislation which stated very explicitly the conditions which were to be present before the bishop could be allowed to divide a parish.[24] Such a statement of the causes seemed to imply some customary practice prior to this very explicit legislation. The Council of Toulouse stated that the bishop had the power to perform this act, but bound him to obtain the consent of his chapter of canons before acting. Seemingly, at least, the Council of Toulouse merely tolerated the division of a parish when it was impossible for parishioners to come regularly to the parish church.

[21] Funk (1840-1907), *Lehrbuch der Kirchengeschichte* (2 vols., increased and revised by Karl Bihlmeyer (+ 1942), Paderborn, 1921), I, 400.

[22] *Caroli I Capitulare ad Salisburgum*, can. 3—*Monumenta Germaniae Historica, Leges*, I (ed. Pertz, Hannoverae, 1835), p. 24 (hereafter cited *MGH*); *Caroli I Excerpt. Canon.*, can. 19—*MGH, Leges*, I, 254; *Ansigisi Capit.*, lib. 2, n. 45—*MGH, Leges*, I, 299; Council of Mayence (847), c. 11—Hardouin (1646-1729), *Acta Conciliorum et Epistolae Decretales ac Constitutiones Summorum Pontificium* (12 vols., Parisiis, 1714-1715), V, 10. (Hereafter cited Hardouin.)

[23] C. 41: "Ecclesiae antiquitus constitutae nec decimis, nec ulla possessione priventur, ita ut novis oratoriis tribuantur."—Mansi, XIV, 74.

[24] Council of Toulouse (843 or 844), c. 7: ". . . si longitudo itineris, aut periculum aquae aut silvae, aut alicuius certae rationis vel necessitatis causa poposcerit; et si mulierum vel infantium, aut debilium imbecillitas ad ecclesiam principalem non possit occurrere, . . ."—*MGH, Leges*, I, 279; Hardouin, IV, 1459.

The Council of Arles (813) as also the Council of Mainz (813) had adverted to the fact that ancient churches were not to be deprived of their income when new churches were erected.[25] Commenting on this statement Gratian (+ ca. 1157) stated that a bishop could divide a parish subject to him into two churches with the consent of his clerics, and that once the division had been accomplished the new church was absolved from all obligations to the older church. He emphasized that unless this were so there would be a multitude of churches without any real rights.[26] The Council of Tribur (895), becoming even more specific, stated that a new parish church should be at least four miles removed from the parochial church from which it was divided.[27]

In the light of the words *consentiente episcopo* in the canon, it appears that although the bishop had the last word in determining whether or not a new parish was to be erected by means of a division, the initiative could lie with others. This council was held at the time when many of the churches were in the hands of owners of large estates, and it evidently had in mind the fact that the landowners could and did begin such transactions. In view of this the Fathers of the council cautiously demanded the consent of the bishop, while at the same time they legislated concerning the distance which should separate parish churches. In mentioning the need of qualified priests who were to be appointed to the new parishes, the council brought out the great problem confronting bishops who had to deal with some landowners who were inclined to assert for themselves powers reserved to the bishops, and also

---

[25] C. 20—Mansi, XIV, 62.

[26] C. 53, C. XVI, q. 1.

[27] Can. 14: "Placuit huic sancto concilio, ut secundum sanctiones canonum, decimae, sicut et aliae possessiones, antiquis conserventur ecclesiis, sicut in Chalcedonensi sancto concilio statutum est. . . . Si quis autem in affinitate antiquae ecclesiae novalia rura excoluerit, decima exinde debita antiquae reddatur ecclesiae. Si vero in qualibet silva, vel deserto loco, ultra milliaria quattuor aut quinque, vel eo amplius, aliquod dirutum collaboraverit, et illic consentiente episcopo ecclesiam construxerit, et consecratam perpetraverit, prospiciat presbyterium ad servitium Dei idoneum et studiosum, et tunc demum novan decimam novae reddat ecclesiae; salva tamen potestate episcopi."—Mansi, XVIII A, 140.

confirmed the traditional determination of the Church to provide the best possible care for the faithful.

Gratian commented on an early decretal letter which referred to the ease with which the Holy See consecrated new bishops when the needs of the faithful demanded an increase in the episcopacy.[28] He observes that inasmuch as from one diocese two could be made, so also from one parish two could be established where only one had existed before. Proceeding to reaffirm the necessity of getting the consent of the clerics who formed the bishop's council, he maintained that the parishioners of the new church were absolved from any obligations to the old church.[29]

The reluctance of the Church to allow the division of minor benefices was demonstrated on several occasions in the twelfth century. A letter of Pope Gregory IX (1227-1241) to the Archbishop of Tours demanded that a certain *praebenda,* which was not a parish, had to be restored to its erstwhile status on the score that there was no cause for the division.[30] The Glossator observed that as a general rule a praebend was not to be divided, and that if one had been divided without a cause, then those who were responsible for the division had to restore it to its former status.[31] Commenting

---

[28] C. 53, C. XVI, q. 1: "Praecipimus, ut iuxta sacrorum canonum statuta, ubi multitudo excrevit fidelium, ex vidore Apostolicae Sedis debeas ordinare episcopos, pia tamen contemplatione, ut non vilescat dignitas episcopatus." Jaffé records this letter under n. 2239.

[29] C. 53, C. XVI, q. 1, *dictum*: "Sicut duo episcopatus . . . in unum possunt redigi, et unus in duobus valet dividi; sic etiam episcopus de baptismalibus, et parochianis ecclesiis facere potest cum consensu suorum clericorum. Quod cum factum fuerit, illa pars populi, quae novis ecclesiis supponitur, a iure prioris ecclesiae absolvitur. Hoc nisi fieri posset, multitudo ecclesiarum ad paucitatem redigeretur. Plures autem baptismales ecclesias in una terminatione facere non potest."

[30] C. 36, X, *de praebendis et dignitatibus,* III, 5; Potthast (1824-1898), *Regesta Pontificum Romanorum inde ab anno post Christum natum MCXCVIII ad annum MCCCIV* (2 vols., Berolini, 1874-1875), n. 9630 (hereafter cited Potthast).

[31] *Glossa* on c. 36, X, *de praebendis et dignitatibus,* III, 5: "Maioribus ecclesiae beneficiis in sua integritate manentibus indecorum nimis videtur, ut minorum clericorum praebendae patiantur sectionem. Idcirco, ut, sicut in magnis, ita quoque in minimis membris suis firmatam ecclesia habeat unitatem, divisionem praebendarum aut dignitatum permutationem fieri prohibemus."

on this canon Panormitanus (1386-1453) stated that the Council wished to indicate a negative rule relative to the change in status of all benefices, namely, that there was to be no change unless a just cause was present, and that it was to be accomplished through the authority of the proper superiors.[32]

Any misapprehension concerning the application of the earlier law on the division of benefices, and especially of parishes, was definitely removed about the year 1170, when Pope Alexander III (1159-1181) sent a most important letter to the Archbishop of York, in England. This document, mandatory in form, took into account not only the distance many parishioners had to travel to the parish church, but also the fact that during winter many could not make the dangerous journey, and commanded the division of the parish. The Pope applied the principles which had been set down by Council of Toulouse in this matter.[33]

Besides the elements taken from the canon of this council, there were many additional factors in the letter, factors which were to serve as guides for all bishops in the future. It was mindful of the rich revenues of the old parish, making reference to the fact that the mother church would suffer no harmful loss when the new parish began to live independently. It stated that the incumbent pastor had no right to interfere with the division. Furthermore, it attributed all future revenues from the village to the new church, and indicated that a satisfactory endowment was to be granted to it. The bishop alone was authorized to effect the division.[34]

---

[32] *Commentaria in Quinque Libros Decretalium* (5 vols. in 8, Venetiis, 1588), Lib. III, tit. 5, n. 8 (hereafter cited Panormitanus).

[33] Council of Toulouse, c. 7—Hardouin, IV, 1459.

[34] "Ad audientium nostram noveris pervenisse, quod villa, quae dicitur H., tantum perhibetur ab ecclesia parochiali distare, ut *in* tempore hiemali, quum pluviae inundant, non possint parochiani sine magna difficultate ipsam adire, unde non valent congruo tempore ecclesiasticis officiis interesse. Quia igitur dicta ecclesia ita dicitur *in* reditibus abundare, quod praeter illius villae proventus minister illius convenienter valeat sustentationem habere, *fraternitati tuae per apostolica scripta mandamus,* quatenus, si res ita se habet, ecclesiam ibi aedifices, et in ea sacerdotem, sublato appellationis obstaculo, ad praesentationem rectoris ecclesiae maioris cum canonico fundatoris assensu institutas, ad sustentationem suam eiusdem villae obventiones ecclesiasticas percepturum, providens tamen, ut competens in ea honor pro

It is to be noted that the rector retained the right of presentation, if he wished, but in the event that he rebelled against the command, the bishop was to appoint a suitable priest to the new post. Although this letter assumed immense importance almost immediately, that importance became universal when this decretal letter was included in the official collection of Gregory IX, thereby becoming authentic law which bound the whole Church.

In the thirteenth century Pope Innocent III (1198-1216) wrote to the Archbishop of Turin a letter in which the question of the validity of the division of a praebend vacant at the time the division occurred was treated. The Pope restated the teaching of the Council of Tours (1163) that no division of praebends was to take place, but added the important qualifying note that a division in that particular instance would be valid and licit so long as sufficient revenue was forthcoming to support the incumbents of the two praebends. Although the case did not concern the division of a parish, the Pontiff applied the principles which related to the division of any minor benefice.[35]

In his gloss on this decretal letter Panormitanus argued that four conditions needed to be fulfilled before any one praebend could be divided into two or more. First, it had to be evident that the division had to be intended by the one who effected it. Secondly, the consent of the chapter was necessary, for whenever the status of the Church

---

facultate loci matrici ecclesiae servetur, quod quidem fieri posse videtur, quum eiusdem villae dominus viginti acras terrae frugiferae velit impedire, tu nihilominus facias idem opus ad perfectionem deduci, et virum bonum appellationis cessante diffugio instituere non omittas."—c. 3, X, *de ecclesiis aedificandis vel reparandis,* III, 48; Jaffé, n. 13884.

[35] "Vacante quadam praebenda in ecclesia tua, duas ex ea constituens, ad illas de consensu capituli tui duos canonicos assumpsisti, quorum altero viam universae carnis ingresso, praebendam, quam defunctus habuerat, quidam clericus nomine Hippolytus fuit auctoritate sedis Apostolicae assecutus. Verum cum idem Hippolytus te super integritate praebendae per quasdam nostras literas inquietet, et alius idem ius adversus te se habere proponat, quid facere debeas requisisti. Super quo sic diximus respondendum, quod, cum Turonensis statuta concilii sectionem inhibeant praebendarum, teneris utrique de his, quae vacare contigerit, integrare praebendam, nisi rationabili causa de vacante supradicta praebenda duae fuerint constitutae, ac tot sint utriusque proventus, quod per utramque sit utrique provisum in beneficio competenti."—c. 26, X, *de praebendis et dignitatibus,* III, 5; *Potthast,* n. 4847.

was changed or altered such a consent was always demanded. In the third place there had to be a reasonable cause. And the fourth condition was that the income from each praebend had to be sufficient to provide the sustenance to which the incumbents were entitled.[36] Panormitanus made the further observation that the Holy Father did not demand that all praebends must be equal, but that each have a sufficient revenue for the proper support of the cleric in charge.[37]

Pope Gregory IX (1227-1241) demonstrated in a letter to the bishop of Brescia that the division of minor benefices was still a serious matter, since it was against the prescription of the Council of Tours. While the Pope indeed was not dealing with the division of a parish, yet he applied the principles which were in use in all cases wherein division of minor benefices was concerned.[38] Gratian had observed in his comment (*dictum*) on a canon discussed above that the consent of the clerics involved was neccessary when a division of baptismal or parochial churches was concerned.[39] In the case that was brought to the attention of Pope Gregory IX it appeared that the clerics were willing to agree to the division. Yet, since there were no canonical causes which warranted the division, the Pope ordered the recall of the division that had been made so that the original praebend was restored to its earlier status.

From this period until the Council of Trent the legislation was quite stable, with the bishops universally throughout the Church following especially the law which had been borrowed from the ordinance of Pope Alexander III.[40] All further legislation was concerned with a more definite explanation of the nature of the canon-

---

[36] *Commentaria,* Lib. III, tit. 5, n. 26.

[37] *Loc. cit.;* c. 6, X, *de constitutionibus,* I, 2.

[38] "Quum saepe contingat, quod ad unam praebendam duo clerici propter nimiam importunitatem petentium eligantur, utrum confirmanda sit talis electio, vel potius irritanda; nos igitur attendentes, quod, si duo unam praebendam tenerent, illud esset sectionem, et, si unus illorum ipsam obtineret praebendam, sub expectatione alius contra Lateranensis concilii statuta remaneret, inquisitione tuae taliter respondemus, quod talis electio de rigore iuris penitus est cassanda."—c. 20, X, *de praebendis et dignitatibus,* III, 5: Potthast, n. 2656.

[39] C. 53, C. XVI, q. 1, *dictum.* Cf. *supra,* p. 10.

[40] Cf. *supra,* pp. 12-13.

ical cause. For all practical purposes the causes were regarded as reducible to these: the necessity or the utility of the Church and the increase in the number of the faithful.[41]

Direct reference was made to the division of parishes under the care of religious in a letter from Pope Alexander III (1159-1181) to the canons regular and the monks of the diocese of York in England.[42] The glossator observed that religious could divide parishes with the consent of the bishop.[43] This letter very obviously sought to correct abuses which had taken place in Britain. It reaffirmed the ancient teaching of the Church that all the faithful in a diocese are under the care of the bishop. The tenor of the letter was such that the only conclusion which could be drawn was that the power to divide parishes, whether under the care of diocesan priests or of religious, belonged exclusively to the bishop. Since this emphatic denial of the right to divide their parishes was later incorporated in the Decretals of Gregory IX, it formed part of the universal law of the Church and was to continue as such until the time of the Council of Trent (1545-1563).

An examination of these early laws of the Church in regard to the division of parishes points to the fact that change was held in considerable disfavor. The reasons were clear enough. Inasmuch as established parishes were loath to part with the material resources which rightfully belonged to them, it was not difficult to understand the reluctance of the pastors who were attached to the parishes to give up some of their income. But even more important among the reasons for hesitancy on the part of the Popes and

[41] C. 4, *de privilegiis,* V, 7, in VI°; c. 1, *de concessione praebendae et ecclesiae non vacantis,* IV, in Extravag. Ioan. XXII.

[42] ". . . mandamus, quatenus, si quas portiones vel antiquos reditus clericorum indebite sine consilio vel consensu archiepiscopi vestri, postquam ipse archiepiscopatum habuerit, minuere vel parochias dividere praesumpsistis, eas ad integritatem pristinam revocetis, et rationabiles et antiquas pensiones clericorum, qui debent altaribus deservire, integras et illibatas servetis, et in eclesiis de quibus certas eis pensiones soliti estis percipere, portiones vel antiquos reditus, quos in illis clerici ante tempora ipsius archiepiscopi et postquam adeptus est archiepiscopatum habuerant, nullatenus praesumptione temeraria minuatis, ne parochias ecclesiarum auctoritate vestra dividere aliquatenus praesumatis."—c. 10, X, *de praebendis et dignitatibus,* III, 5; Jaffé, n. 13892.

[43] Glossa ad c. 10, X, *de praebendis et dignitatibus,* III, 5, s.v. *redditus.*

bishops was the concept of perpetuity as of the very nature of a benefice.

To forestall all hasty action on the part of bishops, certain requisites or causes were demanded before a division could be effected. The good of souls was the chief concern. But once it was established that only through a division could the faithful receive the proper care, then the effecting of a division became mandatory. Custom apparently had paved the way for the first written law enacted by the Council of Toulouse (843 or 844). Later councils then established the causes which canonically warranted a division of the older parishes, and indicated the manner in which the admissible division was to be accomplished.

CHAPTER II

The Division of Parishes Since the Council of Trent

Article 1. Pertinent Legislation

The Council of Trent found that the ordinance of Alexander III, which became universal law through its inclusion in the Decretals of Gregory IX,[1] contained the most satisfactory group of norms for the guidance of bishops when they deemed it necessary to divide parishes. Reaffirming the law as set down in that important letter, the Fathers of the Council added some necessary regulations concerning the support of the priests who became appointed to the new parishes. They insisted that the bishop set aside a suitable portion of the income of the mother church for that purpose, no matter under what title this income pertained to that church. Furthermore, the bishop was empowered to enforce the making of contributions on the part of people when such contributions were found necessary for the sustenance of the clergy of the new parish.[2]

---

[1] C. 3, X, *de ecclesiis aedificandis et reparandis,* III, 48.

[2] "Episcopi, etiam tanquam apostolicae sedis delegati, in omnibus ecclesiis parochialibus vel baptismalibus, in quibus populus ita numerosus sit, ut unus rector non possit sufficere ecclesiasticis sacramentis ministrandis et cultui divino peragendo, cogant rectores, vel alios, ad quos pertinet, sibi tot sacerdotis ad hoc munus adiungere, quot sufficiant ad sacramenta exhibenda et cultum divinum celebrandum. In iis vero, in quibus ob locorum distantiam sive difficultatem parochiani sine magno incommodo ad percipienda sacramenta et divina officia audienda accedere non possunt, novas parochias etiam invitis rectoribus iuxta formam constitutionis Alexandri III, quae incipit: *Ad audientiam,* constituere possint. Illis autem sacerdotibus, qui de novo erunt ecclesiis noviter erectis praeficiendi, competens assignetur portio arbitrio episcopi ex fructibus ad ecclesiam matricem quomodocunque pertinentibus, et, si necesse fuerit, compellere possit populum ea subministrare, quae sufficiant ad vitam dictorum sacerdotum sustentandam; quacunque reservatione generali vel speciali vel affectione super dictis ecclesiis non obstantibus. Neque huiusmodi ordinationes et erectiones possint tolli nec impediri ex quibuscunque provisionibus, etiam vigore resignationis, aut quibusvis aliis derogationibus vel suspensionibus."—Conc. Trident., sess. XXI, *de ref.,* c. 4.

A study of this decree reveals the desire of the Council to give the bishops power sufficient to safeguard adequately the souls entrusted to them. In another decree the same council commanded that parishes be established wherever possible, especially in its reference to those cities and localities where parochial churches had no definite boundaries.[3]

Since the people were required to receive the sacraments from their proper pastors, it was fundamental that they have proper parishes, and the Council was determined that bishops should act promptly to gain this goal. Considered together with the other decrees, this legislation manifests the determination of the Council to protect the faithful, to give them ample opportunity to receive the sacraments, to give them a proper pastor responsible for their care, and to divide benefices of a parochial nature when that would effect the purposes outlined.

It is to be noted that bishops received both ordinary and delegated power to divide parishes.[4] An analysis of this power will be made in the next section. It suffices for the present to state that bishops acted by virtue of their ordinary power when dividing secular parishes, and as delegates of the Holy See when dividing the parishes which were under the care of religious.[5]

While the Council of Trent did not legislate directly concerning the division of religious parishes, it is apparent from the fact that no exemptions were made in the law, as well as from the added clause, *etiam tanquam apostolicae sedis delegati,* that the power to

---

[3] ". . . In iis quoque civitatibus ac loci, ubi parochiales ecclesiae certos non habet fines, nec earum rectores proprium populum, quem regant, sed promiscue petentibus sacramenta administrantur, mandat sancta synodus episcopis pro tutiori animarum eis commissarum salute, ut distincto populo in certas propriasque parochias unicuique suum perpetuum peculiaremque parochum assignent, qui eas cognoscere valeat, et a quo solo licite sacramenta suscipiant, aut alio ultiori modo, prout loci qualitas exegerit, provideant. Idemque in iis civitatibus ac locis, ubi nullae sunt parochiales, quam primum fieri curent, non obstantibus quibuscunque privilegiis ac consuetudinibus, etiam immemorabilibus."—Conc. Trident., sess. XXIV, *de ref.*, c. 13.

[4] "Episcopi, etiam tanquam apostolicae sedis delegati. . ."—Sess. XXI, *de ref.*, c. 4.

[5] De Luca, *Theatrum Veritatis et Iustitiae* (16 vols., Coloniae Agrippinae, 1576), Vol. I, pars 1, disc. 12, n. 8.

divide such parishes was included in the legislation. Further strengthening this contention was the practice which grew out of the earlier Decretal law in that regard.[6] Again, legislation concerning religious and the care of souls demonstrated that the bishop had wide powers over all things relating to parishes controlled by religious.[7]

In view of this legislation it can be easily that the Council was in no way desirous of changing the earlier law. Rather, it aimed at bringing the older legislation sharply into focus with a view to correcting existing abuses while at the same time clarifying the position of the bishop in regard to religious who had the care of souls. The Fathers of the Council decreed that those who exercised the care of souls were subject to the bishop immediately in all things that pertained to that *cura animarum,* regardless of their secular or religious status.[8]

ARTICLE 2. EARLY INTERPRETATION OF TRIDENTINE LAW CONCERNING THE DIVISION OF PARISHES

Since the present law of the Code is practically identical with the pre-Code law as it was promulgated by the Council of Trent, and since the Tridentine law was merely an amplification and clarification of the earlier Decretal legislation, a brief discussion of the early interpretation is necessary for a more complete understanding of the present law. Older commentators discussed the division of parishes by combining the decree of Alexander III and the regulations given by the Council.[9] While much of the interpre-

[6] ". . . ne parochias ecclesiarum auctoritate vestra dividere aliquatenus praesumatis."—c. 10, X, *de praebendis et dignitati bus,* III, 5.

[7] "In monasteriis seu domibus virorum seu mulierum, quibus imminet animarum cura personarum saecularium, praeter eas, quae de illorum monasteriorum seu locorum familia, personae tam regulares quam saeculares huiusmodi curam exercentes subsint immediate in iis, quae ad dictam curam et sacramentorum administrationem pertinent, iurisdictione, visitationi et correctioni episcopi, in cuius dioecesi sunt sita. Nec ibi aliqui etiam ad nutum amovibilis deputentur, nisi de eiusdem consensu, ac praevio examine per eum aut eius vicarium faciendo; . . ."—Conc. Trident., sess. XXV, *de regularibus,* c. 11.

[8] *Loc. cit.*

[9] Compare c. 3, X, *de ecclesiis aedificandis vel reparandis,* III, 48, with Conc. Trident., sess. XXI, *de ref.,* c. 4.

tation which the decretalists furnished can be applied to the present law, there are several important differences which must be discussed. First to be considered here are the rigorous conditions which were demanded before a division was deemed permissible. Then to be analyzed are the following factors: the nature of the power used by bishops in their dividing of parishes, the rôle of the chapter in this matter, and the means of support for the newly created parishes.

In the Council of Trent, the Fathers, following the old legal provision that the division of a benefice was always to be regarded as an adverse item,[10] insisted first that when the faithful became so numerous as to preclude a proper spiritual care by the pastor alone, "the bishops shall . . . compel the rectors or those to whom it pertains, to associate with themselves in this office as many priests as are necessary to administer the sacraments and carry on divine worship."[11]

Garcia (+ 1645) cited an early Rota decision which reechoed the statement of the Council that the bishops could compel pastors to accept assistants to administer the sacraments and to perform the sacred rites.[12] Other decretalists agreed that the division of a parish was a subsidiary remedy which was not to be applied until all other measures were found unsuited to the extant need.[13] Con-

---

[10] Panormitanus (Nicholaus de Tudeschis, 1386-1453) wrote in the fifteenth century: "Non enim debet sine causa parochia ecclesiae dividi. Est enim ista alienatio iurium ecclesiae quae sine causa fieri non debet."—*Lectura in Lib. III Decretalium,* c. III, tit. 48, n. 2. In a similar vein Cardinal De Luca had written: "Per erectionem (novae) depauperetur antiqua ecclesia paroecialis, eiusque dignitas vilesceret."—*Theatrum Veritatis et Iustitiae,* Vol. III, pars II, *De Decimis,* disc. 12, n. 8.

[11] Sess. XXI, *de ref.,* c. 4—Schroeder, *Canons and Decrees of the Council of Trent* (St. Louis: B. Herder, 1941), p. 138.

[12] *In Tyrassonen.,* 6 iun. 1594—*De Beneficiis Ecclesiasticis Amplissimus et Doctissimus Tractatus* (Venetiis, 1618), P. XII, c. 3, n. 10. A similar decision, but somewhat later, *in Ostunen.,* 12 iul. 1631, is cited by Barbosa (1589-1649), *Summa Apostolicarum Decisionum—Collectanea Doctorum in varia Concilii Tridentini Decreta et Canones* (Lugduni, 1657), P. II, n. 1.

[13] Fagnanus (1598-1678), *Commentaria super Quinque Libros Decretalium* (4 vols., Venetiis, 1697), Lib. III, tit. 48, c. 3, n. 23; Schmalgrueber, Lib. III, tit. 48, n. 9; Pirhing (1606-1679), *Jus Canonicum in V Libros Decretalium distributum* (5 vols., Venetiis, 1659-1677), Lib. III, tit. 48, § 2, n. 10.

sequently, in parishes, religious or secular, which had so great a number of parishioners that they were unable to give the desired care, the addition of other priests who resided in auxiliary churches strategically placed in the parish, or with the pastor, was preferable to a division, even in cases wherein other causes seemed to warrant the division of the parish.[14]

The Council of Trent had stated that "in those (churches) . . . to which, by reason of distance and hardship, the parishioners cannot come without grave inconvenience to receive the sacraments and hear the divine offices, they (the bishops) may, even against the will of the rectors, establish new churches, pursuant to the form of the constitution of Alexander III, which begins "*Ad audientiam.*"[15] The decretalists discussed this part of the decree at great length, searching out the precise reasons which permitted or demanded the division of a parish in a given case. They established certain principles which are found later to have guided the Rota and the Sacred Congregation of the Council in determining the validity of some of the effected divisions.[16] The causes which the Council of Trent had designated in a general way were summed up briefly as those of distance and hardship, if either of these resulted in grave inconvenience to the people. The Council left it to the judgment of the bishop to determine when these causes existed. Difficulty of approach to the church could arise because of natural obstacles which at certain times of the year rendered approach to the church impossible.[17] The application of these principles will be seen more fully in the canonical commentary.

Barbosa stated that the same principles were to be used to

---

[14] Monacellus (+ 1715), *Formulare Legale Practicum Fori Ecclesiastici* (3. ed., 4 vols. in 3, Romae, 1844), I, tit. 2, form. 3, n. 4 (hereafter cited *Formulare Legale*).

[15] Sess. XXI, *de ref.*, c. 4—Schroeder, *Canons and Decrees of the Council of Trent*, p. 138.

[16] E.g. S.C.C., *In Brixinen.*, 26 ian. 1743—*Thesaurus Resolutionum Sacrae Congregationis Concilii* (167 vols., Romae, 1718-1908), XII, 37, 55, 103 (hereafter cited *Thesaurus*); S.C.C., *Ianuen.*, *Dismembrationis*, 25 ian. 1879—*Thesaurus*, CXXXVIII (1879), 56-65.

[17] Ferraris, *Bibliotheca Canonica, Iuridica, Moralis, Theologica necnon Ascetica, Polemica, Rubristica, Historica* (9 vols., Romae, 1885-1899), II, s.v. *Dismembratio*, n. 14 (hereafter cited *Bibliotheca*).

determine the existence of canonical causes for a division whether the parish was subject to regulars or diocesan priests.[18]

The nature of the power conceded to bishops by the Council of Trent was considered quite fully by all the early commentators. They were unanimous in agreeing that the bishop acted with ordinary power when dividing parishes under the care of religious priests, and that he acted as a delegate of the Holy See when he divided religious parishes.[19] This was held to be true because exempt regulars were responsible only to the Holy See for their property. As the Council had insisted upon the right of bishops to oversee everything concerned with the *cura animarum,*[20] the decretalists concluded logically that, unlike the secular parishes, no consent of the chapter was necessary when the division of a religious parish was decided upon by the bishop.[21] When the bishop acted as a delegate of the Holy See such a consent was not demanded, since the bishop was in such a case acting for the Pope who himself was not bound by any such restriction.[22]

The division of secular parishes, on the other hand, did require the consent of the chapter, since a division constituted a species of alienation.[23] Since the Council of Trent was silent on the matter, as was also the constitution of Alexander III, Schmalzgrueber argued that in this case the earlier law had not been changed, that there a kind of alienation involved in division, and hence that the

---

[18] *De officio et potestate Episcopi* (2 vols., Romae, 1656), II, P. III, alleg. 68, n. 4.

[19] Cf. Schmalzgrueber, lib. III, tit. 48, n. 20, for an example of the argument.

[20] "In monasteries . . . those persons . . . who exercise that *cura* (*animarum*) shall in all things that pertain to that *cura* and to the administration of the sacraments be subject immediately to the jurisdiction, visitation, and correction of the bishop in whose diocese they are located."—sess. XXV, *de regularibus,* c. 11—Schroeder, *Canons and Decrees of the Council of Trent,* p.

[21] Schmalzgrueber, lib. III, tit. 48, n. 20.

[22] *Loc. cit.*

[23] Fagnanus, lib. III, tit. 48, c. 3, n. 51; Reiffenstuel, lib. III, tit. 48, n. 20; Pirhing, lib. III, tit. 48, c. 3, n. 10.

Schmalzgrueber refers to a letter of Gregory I, contained in c. 7, X, *de donationibus,* III, 24—Potthast, n. 2350—to support his contention that alienation was involved in the act of effecting a division, since through it the rights and very often also the revenues of the mother church were diminished.

consent of the chapter was necessary for valid action in this respect.[24]

Once the parish had been divided, there remained the problem of sufficient support for the priests assigned to the new parish. The Council of Trent determined that the bishop was to give them a "suitable portion . . . from the fruits in whatever way belonging to the mother-church, and if it is necessary, he may compel the people to contribute what may be sufficient for the sustenance of those priests."[25]

If the church was endowed by some person or persons to such a degree that no other sources of income were necessary, the mother church was considered absolved from all obligations in that regard.[26] But in the absence of such an endowment the bishop received authority from the Council to allocate a portion of the income of the mother church to the newly erected church, first ascertaining that sufficient funds were left for the proper support of the mother church. The decretalists declared that a sufficient endowment was one which provided all things necessary for the church itself, for the priests assigned to the parish, for the fulfillment of any financial obligations to the bishop, for the care of the poor and the like.[27]

If the mother church was financially unable to give up sources of revenue sufficient to endow the filial church, the Council provided that the bishop should compel the new parishioners to provide the necessary funds. Fagnanus stated that the bishop could enforce his regulations in this matter with opportune remedies.[28] However, when poverty existed among the people, then the duty of providing the endowment fell to those to whom the church was subject *in temporalibus,* such as the abbot of a monastery.[29] When there was no such subjection, or when the imposing of such a duty would

---

[24] *Loc. cit.*

[25] Sess. XXI, *de ref.*, c. 4—Schroeder, *Canons and Decrees of the Council of Trent,* p. 138.

[26] Fagnanus, lib. III, tit. 48, c. 3, n. 5; Schmalzgrueber, lib. III, tit. 48, n. 23.

[27] Schmalzgrueber, lib. III, tit. 48, n. 22.

[28] *Commentaria,* lib. III, tit. 48, c. 3, n. 5.

[29] Fagnanus, *ibid.*, n. 7.

have proved harmful, the bishop himself was required to endow the church.[80]

In consequence of its endowment of the new church, the mother church acquired the right of presentation, a right vested in the rector.[81] If the endowment was attained through contributions from the faithful, or if it was provided by the bishop himself, then none acquired this right.[82]

This brief study of the interpretation of the law as given by the Council of Trent serves indeed as a basis for a study of the present-day regulations, though it has aimed chiefly at showing the differences which exist between the earlier law and the Code. In the canonical commentary which follows, these discrepancies will be seen in clearer detail as they are placed side by side with the new law. Since much of the present law concerning the division of parishes is the same as that given by Pope Alexander III and the Council of Trent, the decretalists must be studied in relation to the modern law, and consequently their interpretations concerning the earlier law insofar as it still continues to regulate the division of parishes will be applied in the proper place in the commentary.

ARTICLE 3. LEGISLATION AFTER THE COUNCIL OF TRENT

The Council of Trent had set down the general norms to be followed in the division of parishes. The commentators had particularized this legislation in such a fashion that bishops found the proper procedure well outlined. Subsequent legislative activity was devoted chiefly to accomplishing the goal of the Council of Trent, namely, that bishops should divide the people into definite and distinct parishes, and assign to each of these parishes its own permanent parish priest.[83]

Several Popes reminded the bishops that the decree of the Council of Trent was still in force,[84] and urged them to avail

[80] Schmalzgrueber, lib. III, tit. 48, n. 24; Fagnanus, *ibid.*, n. 7; Barbosa, *De officio et potestate episcopi*, alleg. 70, n. 29.

[81] Pirhing, lib. III, tit. 48, § II, n. 12.

[82] Fagnanus, lib. III, tit. 48, c. 3, n. 39.

[83] Conc. Trident., sess. XXIV, *de ref.*, c. 13.

[84] Innocentius III, const. *Apostolici ministerii*, 23 maii 1723, n. 14—*Codicis Iuris Canonici cura Emi Petri Card. Gasparri editi* (9 vols., Romae (postea

themselves of the powers given them to divide parishes,[35] in order to attain the ultimate goal of a sufficient number of parishes to provide a maximum pastoral care for souls.[36]

The law of the Council of Trent remained universally binding until the Code, and though the Sacred Congregation of the Council and the Rota were often called upon to interpret the law and to decide questions of fact, there was no introduction of new legislation. The decisions of the Sacred Congregation and of the Rota did much to clarify existing law, and also contributed much which is now part of the present law. The contributions made by both, and the decisions which led to a most helpful jurisprudence, will be seen in the commentary.

SUMMARY

The first positive law regarding the division of parishes was enunciated by the Council of Toulouse in the year 843 or 844. Reasons justifying division were given for the first time. Reduced to their ultimate basis, these could be stated as the necessity and the utility for the division in view of the otherwise ineffective care of souls if no division was made. Restrictions were stated which protected parishes from injudicious or unjust division. Other councils before the Council of Trent listed other reasons as justifying the act of division, but constantly held that a division should be attempted only as a last resort.

A particular constitution of Pope Alexander III became universal law when it was embodied in the Decretals of Gregory IX. It indicated regulations for the division of parishes which continue until the present time. The Council of Trent reaffirmed the law

---

Civitate Vaticana): Typis Polyglottis Vaticanis, 1923-1939 (Vols. VII-IX, ed. cura et studio Emi Iustiniani Seredi). Hereafter cited *Fontes*. Benedictus XII, const. *In supremo,* 23 sept. 1724, n. 11—*Fontes,* n. 283; Benedictus XIV, const. *Ad militantis,* 30 mart 1742, nn. 11 and 16—*Fontes,* n. 326.

[35] Conc. Trident., sess. XXI, *de ref.*, c. 4.

[36] Pallottini, *Collectio omnium conclusionum et resolutionum quae in causis propositis apud Sacram Congregationem Cardinalium S. Concilii Tridentini interpretum prodierunt ab eius institutione anno MDLXIV ad annum MDCCCLX distinctis titulis alphabetico ordine per materias digesta* (18 vols., Romae, 1868-1895), s.v. *Ecclesia parochialis,* III, 6.

of the Decretals, amplifying and clarifying it, in order to impress bishops with the powers that they possessed to cure the ills which beset parish organization at the time.

Since the Council of Trent the Holy See has concerned itself chiefly with applying the law in particular instances by gradually building up the growth of parish units into effective instruments as means for the accomplishment of its divinely commissioned task. The jurisprudence growing out of the solution of practical cases played an important rôle in the evolution of the present law.

PART TWO

Canonical Commentary

CHAPTER III

Definition of Terms

Article 1. Parishes in the Code

In order to avoid confusion and to prepare the way for a practical discussion of the law regarding the division of parishes, it seems proper to define precisely what is meant by the term parish as it is used in the Code today, and also to explain carefully the meaning of division as it will be used throughout this work. Consequently this introductory chapter will treat of parishes in such a way that an analysis of the constitutive elements of a parish will be made, with emphasis on the territorial principle of law which historically governed the Church in her care for souls. Since a later chapter will concern itself with the division of national parishes, some discussion of the nature of such parishes is necessary in this preliminary article. Also brief reference to parishes under the care of religious and Orientals will be made, in preparation for a later commentary.

The Code itself, while not giving a clear definition of the term "parish," does state the constitutive elements of a parish.[1]

From these elements a satisfactory descriptive definition may be obtained: A parish is that distinct portion of a diocese which has its own particular church administered by a proper pastor, whose duty it is to exercise in the internal forum the ordinary jurisdiction which is necessary for the care of souls committed to his care.[2] Four elements, then, are practically always demanded in

[1] Canon 216, §1. "Territorium cuiuslibet dioecesis dividatur in distinctas partes territoriales; unicuique autem parti sua peculiaris ecclesia cum populo determinato est assignanda, suusque peculiaris rector, tanquam proprius eiusdem pastor, est praeficiendus pro necessaria animarum cura." Canon 216, §3: "Partes dioecesis in 1 sunt paroeciae; . . ."

[2] Fanfani, *De Iure Parochorum* (editio altera, Taurini-Romae: Marietti, 1936), n. 1; Beste, *Introductio in Codicem* (editio altera, St. John's Abbey Press, Collegeville, Minn., 1944), p. 225.

a parish erected according to the dictates of law, namely, a definite territory, a specified congregation, a particular church to which the congregation is assigned, and a resident priest as the pastor. An exception is allowed by the law itself in certain well defined instances, which fact precludes the positive declaration that the four requisites are essential to every parish.[3] The Code declares that with an apostolic indult family or personal parishes, as well as the so-called national parishes, may be erected.[4]

In relation to the present work the most important among the four elements are those which are concerned with the distinct territory and the *coetus fidelium* assigned to that territory. In determining a division, as will be seen, the ordinary must primarily concern himself with these two components, and consequently it is necessary to analyze briefly the rôle in parochial organization of a particular portion of a diocese, the territory to be cared for by one pastor and by one church, together with the group of the faithful attached to that territory.

Canon 216, § 1, lists as the first condition of a parish the distinct territorial part of a diocese. In the creation or division of parishes the boundaries must be clearly determined, not only for the purpose of affording certainty to the pastor regarding the people who will be under his jurisdiction, but also with a view to familiarizing the faithful with the location of their parish church. This demands a more or less arbitrary territorial delimitation which depends largely on the number of the faithful residing in a particular locality. But at the same time, since the enactment of the Council of Trent at least, the Church, in order the better to accomplish her divine work, has insisted on definite boundaries which embrace specified groups of people.

In the sixteenth century many parochial churches were still without definite territorial limits, both in the cities and in the rural areas.[5] The Council of Trent in its decree condemned this very imperfect system of parochial care, and aimed at obviating

[3] Ciesluk, *National Parishes in the United States,* The Catholic University of America Canon Law Studies, n. 190 (Washington, D. C.; The Catholic University of America Press, 1944), pp. 3-4.

[4] Canon 216, § 4.

[5] Wernz, *Jus Decretalium,* II, n. 821.

certain abuses concerning the administration and the reception of the sacraments by making it compulsory for bishops to establish definite parish boundaries.[6] From time to time various Popes took occasion to remind bishops that the law of the Council of Trent had not lost any of its force.[6a] The present Code restates the legislation of the Council of Trent concerning the territorial division of parishes,[7] and reiterates the command of the Council that a territorial division be the ordinarily employed means for the estabing of parishes. Furthermore, this emphasis is more clearly seen in the fact that the present law determines the parochial domicile or quasi-domicile of a person by looking to the territory in which he has his residence.[8]

A provision similar to the one initiated in the Council of Trent was later made by the Sacred Congregation for the Propagation the Faith for so-called mission territories. This Congregation decreed that parishes should be established in missionary countries as soon as possible according to the principles of Canon Law, and that wherever this was not immediately possible territorial divisions were to be established and called "missions" or "stations" or "congregations," over which was to be placed a vicar or administrator.[9] These territorial districts in missionary areas, instituted along identical lines with the territorial parish, differed from parishes particularly because of the status of the hierarchical arrangement of which they were a part, and were called quasi-parishes. In other words, the territories under the jurisdiction of vicars and prefects apostolic were divided into parochial units with definite territorial limits designated as quasi-parishes.[10] To-

---

[6] Sess. XXIV, *de ref.*, c. 13.

[6a] Innocentius XIII (1721-1724), const. *Apostolici ministerii,* 23 maii 1723, n. 14—*Fontes,* n. 280; Benedictus XIV (1740-1758), const. *Ad militantis,* 20 mart. 1742, nn. 11 and 16—*Fontes,* n. 326.

[7] Canon 216.

[8] Canon 94, § 1.

[9] S.C. de Prop. Fide, 18 mart. 1881—*Collectanea S. Congregationis de Propaganda Fide* (2 vols., Romae, 1907), n. 1548 (hereafter cited *Coll. S.C.P.F.*); Benedictus XIV, ep. encycl. *Cum semper oblatas,* 19 aug. 1744—*Fontes,* n. 345.

[10] Clemens IX, bulla *Speculatores,* 13 sept. 1659—*Bullarium Pontificium S. Cong. de Prop. Fide.* (ed. s. Bauer, 7 vols. et Index, Romae, 1839-1858), I, 172; S. C. Consist., declar. 1 aug. 1919, n. 1—*Acta Apostolicae Sedis, Commentarium Officiale* (Romae, 1909-), XI (1919), 346 (hereafter cited *AAS*).

day missionary territories are subject to the same regulations as fully organized dioceses in the matter of parochial division,[11] and the quasi-pastors are practically equivalent to pastors in regard to rights and duties,[12] differing only in the stability of their office,[13] in the method of their nomination and in their obligation of applying the *missa pro populo* as frequently as pastors are bound to do so.[14]

Since a territory without any faithful could not constitute a parish in any sense, it is necessary to give some attention to the persons who make up the parish proper. Of vital importance in the division of parishes are the number of parishioners concerned. Speculatively, too, the presence of large numbers of non-Catholics within a parochial territory could be of some import when a modification of one kind or another is contemplated in that parish. The faithful are the chief object of the Church in her efforts to save souls, and hence together with the pastor who is to work for their salvation form the principal part of the parochial institute. The legislation of the present Code provides ample evidence of the concern felt by the Church for those who are committed to her care for teaching and direction.[15]

Thus far it has been seen that the present law of the Church insists on the division of dioceses into parishes with definite boundaries, which parishes are to care for the souls of those who live within the territory as delimited by the proper authority. It is obvious from the wording of canon 216, § 1, that the Church tends to a uniform division of all dioceses into territorial sections called parishes. At the same time, however, she would not be the ever-solicitous mother that she is were she to ignore the fact that men do not always tend to remain in one part of the world, and that as a result small groups of one nation often migrate to other lands of a different culture and language. Whether such moves proceed from political, economic, or personal reasons is of no

[11] Canon 216, § 2.

[12] Canons 461-470.

[13] Canon 454, § 4.

[14] Canons 457 and 306.

[15] For example, canons 1329-1336 stress the importance of the catechetical instruction to be given to children and to adults.

moment, but it is important for the Church's purpose to safeguard the faith of these people. This was recognized as a matter of grave import as early as the thirteenth century when the IV General Council of the Lateran (1215) gave consideration to the problem.[16]

Innocent III (1198-1216) in a practical way dealt with the problem of diverse languages within the same city, and his answer to the difficulty promptly became universal law when it was incorporated into the Decretals of Gregory IX (1227-1241), promulgated in 1234.[17] This law was directed, not at curing the situation, but at making proper provision for it. For bishops who were faced with the difficulty it became the duty to appoint suitable pastors, who knew the language, to care for the persons of diverse tongue.[18] The Council of Trent obliged bishops to provide suitable pastors for the people with a view to explaining the sacraments to them in the vernacular.[19] Hence there was some indication in its enactments that, if all the obligations imposed by the Council of Trent on bishops were to be executed faithfully, then national parishes enjoyed some basis in law for their existence. Necessity and utility were the chief reasons urged by the Council for the establishing of parishes, and consequently through indult or privilege, or through established custom as based on either of the latter, parishes for national groups migrating outside their own habitat continued to exist. This was true despite the unmistakable legislation of the Council which referred to the setting up of parochial divisions as the norm that was thenceforth to guide bishops in their providing for the proper care of souls.[20] The milder interpretations of the causes for the erection of parishes as stated

---

[16] Canon 9—Mansi, XXII, 998; c. 14, X, *de officio iudicis ordinarii,* I, 31.

[17] C. 14, X, *de officio iudicis ordinarii,* I, 31; cf. Cicognani, *Canon Law* (2. ed. revised, Westminster, Md.; Newman Bookshop, 1946), p. 299.

[18] Gonzalez-Tellez, *Commentaria Perpetua in Singulos Textus Quinque Librorum Decretalium Gregorii IX* (5 vols., Maceratae, 1761), I, tit. XXXI, c. 14; Hostiensis, *In Quinque Decretalium Libros Commentaria* (5 vols. in 3, Venetiis, 1581), I, tit. *de officio iudicis ordinarii,* c. 14, n. 1.

[19] Sess. V, *de ref.,* c. 2; sess. XXII, *de sacrificio missae,* c. 8; sess. XXIII, *de ref.,* c. 1; sess. XXIV, *de ref.,* cc. 4, 7, 18.

[20] Ciesluk, *National Parishes in the United States,* p. 25.

by the Council of Trent[21] led to a sudden growth of national parishes in the late nineteenth and early twentieth century.[22]

Today, as in the enactments of the Council of Trent, it is indeed the existence of territorial parishes that is considered in law as the normal thing, but further express provision is at the same time made for the existence of national parishes.[23] Although fundamentally a national parish exists without reference to territory, it can also be understood in a wider sense as a mixed parish, namely, as one which has the character of a national parish, since it has been established primarily for a national group, and as one which also extends over one or more territorial parishes. This situation obtains when two or more national parishes exist in one city and when concomitantly there have been set certain limits within which the pastors of these parishes may exercise their jurisdiction.[24]

With reference to mixed personal or national parishes, then, bishops are not authorized either to create or to innovate them, and in that distinctive note lies the fundamental difference between them and territorial parishes. Together with the personal or national element, these parishes have the unique distinction of being under the care of the Holy See insofar as their status is concerned. And in these parishes the Holy See manifests its adaptability to all types of situations, precisely in view of the fact that there is a question of such an essential institution as the parish.

Parishes under the care of religious have their own particular characteristics. That fact warrants some added attention in the discussion of the Code law regarding such parishes. In their

[21] *Acta Sanctae Sedis* (Romae, 1865-1908), X (1877), 271-272 (hereafter cited *ASS*); S.R.R., *in causa Bobien., Dismembrationis,* 4 mart. 1911, coram R.P.D. Michaele Lega, Dec. XI, nn. 2, 9, 10—*Decisiones,* III (1911), 105, 109, 110.

[22] Ciesluk, *op. cit., loc. cit.*

[23] Canon 216, § 4.

[24] Coronata, *Institutiones Iuris Canonici* (5 vols., Vols. I-II, 2. ed., 1939; Vols. III-V, 1933-1936, Taurini, Marietti), II, n. 972; Vermeersch-Creusen, *Epitome Iuris Canonici* (6. ed., 3 vols., Mechliniae, Romae: Dessain, 1937-1946), II, n. 533 (hereafter cited *Epitome*); Beste, *Introductio in Codicem,* p. 227.

essential elements secular and religious parishes are identical. But because of the special regulations which relate to the prospective fact of their division, it is proper that some consideration be given them at this point.

Very often the term "religious parish" is used in a broad sense to signify a parish which in any way has come under the care of some particular religious institute. It is noteworthy, however, that the Code reserves the phrase "religious parish" to but one type of parish united to a religious institute.[25] That union is called a union with full right (*pleno iure*), and occurs when the parish is united to the religious institute in such a way that the institute itself becomes the permanent (*habitualis*) pastor, and an actual vicar, who is himself a member of the institute, is therefore nominated by his superior for approval and appointment by the bishop. The parish is not entirely exempted from the power of the local ordinary, for it remains subject to his jurisdiction, visitation, and coercive power, in matters pertaining to the care of souls.[26]

The most complete type of union (*plenissimo iure*) exists when episcopal or quasi-episcopal jurisdiction over the clergy and the people is transferred from the diocesan local ordinary to the abbot of the monastery to which the parish is united. This type of union is to be found in the union of a parish with a territorially independent abbacy.

A third kind of union (*ad temporalia tantum,* or *semi-pleno iure*) is that which occurs when a religious house shares only in the revenues of the parochial endowment and thus gains a material benefit while the administration of the temporalities rests with a priest who has been selected from the secular clergy. This kind of parish is secular, not religious, in character.

Finally, the care of a parish may be committed to the care of religious without being united in any way to the religious community. The parish remains secular, although its actual administration is in the hands of a religious pastor, both in its temporal and in its spiritual affairs.[27]

---

[25] Canon 1425, § 2.

[26] Canon 452; cf. also 456, 1425, § 2, and 471, § 1.

[27] Connolly, *The Canonical Erection of Parishes,* The Catholic University of America Canon Law Studies, n. 114 (Washington, D. C.: The Catholic University of America, 1938), p. 100.

Canon 215, § 1, reserves to the Holy See the *plenissimo iure* effected union of a parish with a religious institute, and an indult of the Holy See is likewise necessary before a union which exists *pleno iure* can be effected by a bishop.[28]

Since the task of administering the care of souls in a diocese rests normally with the secular clergy, the Code restates the earlier law that new parishes are to be secular, even when their institution results from the partition of a religious parish.[29] Religious parishes are recognized by the law as having a place in the Church's economy, and in given circumstances can be erected under the law, as the canons referred to indicate.

Diversity of rites among the population of a country has given rise to the formation of parishes dedicated specifically to the service of the faithful who belong to these rites. Many pronouncements of the Popes during the past centuries and in recent times have insisted on the preservation of the rites and customs of Orientals living among Latins or among other Orientals who follow a different rite.[30] The term "rite" can be defined as the proper manner in which liturgical functions and ceremonies are to be performed.[31] Juridically, however, this definition needs amplification, since it is merely liturgical by nature, and should include as well all the proper sacred functions and the hierarchical constitution

---

[28] Canon 452, § 1.

[29] Canon 1427, § 5. Cf. S.C.C., *Brixinen.*, 16 febr., 16 mart. 1743—*Fontes*, n. 3548.

[30] Benedictus XIV, const. *Etsi pastoralis*, 26 maii 1742—*Fontes*, n. 328; Pius IX, const. *Romani Pontifices*, 6 ian. 1862—*Fontes*, n. 531; litt. encycl. *Amantissimus*, 8 apr. 1862—*Coll. S.C.P.F.*, n. 1226; Leo XIII, const. *Orientalium dignitas*, 30 nov. 1894—*Fontes*, n. 627; Benedictus XV, motu proprio *Dei Providentis*, 1 maii 1917—*AAS*, IX (1917), 529; Pius XI, litt. encycl. *Ecclesia Dei*, 12 nov. 1923—*AAS*, XV (1920), 573.

[31] Wernz-Vidal, *Ius Canonicum ad Codicis Normam Exactum* (7 toms. in 8 vols., Romae: Apud aedes Universitatis Gregorianae, 1923-1938; Tom. II, *De Personis*, 2. ed., 1928; Tom. V, *Ius Matrimoniale*, 2. ed., 1928), II, n. 21 (hereafter cited *Ius Canonicum*); Duskie, *The Canonical Status of Oriental Catholics in the United States*, The Catholic University of America Canon Law Studies, n. 48 (Washington, D. C.: The Catholic University of America, 1928), p. 13.

and discipline binding the faithful under one rule.[32] Briefly, in the Oriental Church, a change of rite implies a change of discipline also, and consequently a change in jurisdiction.

When a Latin bishop finds that the care of souls demands the assistance of an Oriental priest, he must consult with the Sacred Congregation for Orientals to obtain a pastor, or approach one of the Oriental ordinaries in this country if the faithful concerned are under their jurisdiction.[33] Parishes must be erected for these people, and for the same reasons which prompt the Church to institute national parishes, namely, to protect the faith of the people and the beautiful customs which are part of every rite. While there is nothing in the way of Code legislation concerning such parishes, the Holy See has taken care of the problem in several decrees.[34]

This brief summary of the notion of parishes as they are contemplated by the Code will be most helpful to serve as a basis for the discussions occurring throughout the rest of this work. Each type of parish will be viewed with respect to the competent authority for the effecting of a division and to the proper mode of proceeding when the dividing of a parish becomes desirable.

ARTICLE 2. THE NOTION OF THE DIVISION OF PARISHES

The Code takes cognizance of the truly human composition of parishes in several ways, but most particularly in its canons on the modifications which can be made in parishes when certain causes exist.[35] The law recognizes that men move about, that parishes flourish and gradually decline, and that they sometimes cease to exist altogether, and strives to meet all possible contingencies. Canon 1421 lists these modifications which are made necessary by them as transfer of the parochial center of operation from one

[32] Petrani, *De Relatione Iuridica inter Diversos Ritus in Ecclesia Catholica* (Taurini: Marietti, 1930), p. 1.

[33] For a complete treatment of Oriental pastors cf. Ciesluk, *National Parishes in the United States*, pp. 131-136.

[34] Cf. S.C. de Prop. Fide, decr. 1 maii 1897—*Coll. S.C.P.F.*, n. 1966; litt. encycl., 1 oct. 1890—*Coll. S.C.P.F.*, n. 1966, in nota 2; decr. 23 nov. 1940—*AAS*, XXXIII (1941), 28.

[35] Canon 1421.

place to another; dismemberment or the transferring of part of the goods of one parish to another already existing parish; conversion or the change of one type of parish into another; suppression or the complete dissolution of a parish; and division or the constitution of two or more parishes where one existed before. It is with this latter that this work is concerned.

It is to be noted that the Code uses the term "division," as well as the terms designating other forms of modification, in relation to benefices rather than to parishes as such.[36] This is the direct result of the historical basis for division.[37] Since parishes, then as now, were considered to be minor benefices, the application of such principles to them obviously was perfectly legal. Their inclusion in the Code under the title, *De beneficiis ecclesiasticis,* is reason enough to deduce that the ancient legislation concerning parishes as benefices is continued in the present law. Parishes considered as benefices have been discussed by many authors, and need no further discussion from that point of view for the purpose of this work.[38]

Division must be distinguished from dismemberment. The Code defines both terms in canon 1421, which should put an end to the indiscriminate use of the terms. Until the promulgation of the Code dismemberment and division were frequently used as synonymous terms, even in official documents.[39] But the definition given in the law itself now obviates that difficulty.

---

[36] Canon 1421: "translatio beneficii habetur cum beneficii sedes de alio in alium locum deducitur; divisio, cum ex uno duo vel plura beneficia fiunt; dismembratio, cum pars territorii aut bonorum alicuius beneficii ex eodem detrahitur et alii beneficio vel causae piae aut ecclesiastico instituto assignatur; conversio, cum beneficium in aliam speciem mutatur; suppressio, cum prorsus extinguitur."

[37] An example of the application of principles used in the division of benefices to the division of parishes is found in the Council of Mainz (813), c. 41—Mansi, XIV, 74. Cf. also c. 24, C. XVI, q. 3.

[38] Cf. Schmalzgrueber, lib. V, tit. 2; Reiffenstuel, lib. III, tit. 12; Fagnanus, lib. III, tit. 48; Connolly, *The Canonical Erection of Parishes,* pp. 42-44; Mundy, *The Union of Parishes,* pp. 20-41.

[39] S.R.R., *Leodien. Dismembrationis,* 1 febr. 1712—*Decisiones Sacrae Romanae Rotae coram Alexandro Falconerio* (5 vols., Romae (1727-1730), IV, Dec. XXXIV, p. 79; S.C.C., *Lunen. Sarazen., Dismembrationis Paroeciae,* 27 sept. 1732—*Thesaurus,* V (1730-1732), 376; S.C.C., *Cassanen.,* 17 dec. 1740—*Thesaurus,* IX (1739-1740), 101, secundo.

Division, finally, is concerned with the establishment of at least one completely new parish. The fact of the creation of a new moral person severs the new parish territorially from the older parish, and jurisdictionally from subjection to the pastor of the older parish.

CHAPTER IV

Competent Authority for the Division of Parishes

Essential to every ecclesiastical benefice is its institution by some ecclesiastical authority.[1] Consequently, before any official status can be attributed to a benefice, and before it attains to a position entitling it to a status of juridical personality, the proper ecclesiastical authority must designate it as such a benefice.[2] The competent authority for the erection of an ecclesiastical juridical person is the supreme authority of the Church or some other physical or moral person to which the supreme authority has conceded this right. Parishes are ecclesiastical benefices, and consequently follow the rules by which benefices are established. It is of great importance to determine the authority competent to erect parishes by means of division, not only in order to forestall every danger of invalid division, but also in order to facilitate the fact of division in any given circumstance.

Canon 1414, § 1, states that only the Holy See is competent to erect, and thus to modify in any way, consistorial benefices. Such benefices are the dioceses, abbacies and prelacies *nullius,* vicariates and prefectures apostolic.[3] The Roman Pontiff, by reason of his office, can erect any and all benefices.[4] Local ordinaries, on the other hand, are presumed by law to enjoy in their dioceses the right to erect non-consistorial benefices.[5]

The most frequent mode of erection is by way of division,[6] and the canons most pertinent to division reaffirm the law stemming from the decree *Ad audientiam* of Alexander III, written about

[1] Canon 1409. "Beneficium ecclesiasticum est ens iuridicum a competente ecclesiastica auctoritate in perpetuum constitutum seu erectum, constans officio sacro et iure percipiendi reditus ex dote officio adnexos."

[2] Coronata, *Institutiones Iuris Canonici,* II, 972.

[3] Coronata, *Institutiones Iuris Canonici,* II, n. 977; Beste, *Introductio in Codicem,* p. 698.

[4] Canons 218 and 1431.

[5] Canon 1414, § 2. A restriction is placed on this right by canon 394, § 2, where establishment of dignities in a chapter is reserved to the Holy See.

[6] Cf. Connolly, *The Canonical Erection of Parishes,* p. 46.

1170, and vindicating an ordinary power for bishops in the dividing of parishes.[7] Additional delegated powers were conferred by the Council of Trent with a view to enabling bishops to divide parishes held by exempt religious.[8]

In the present law[9] ordinaries have the power to divide any parishes whatsoever (*paroecias quaslibet*). The term local ordinary, according to the prescription of canon 198, § 2, includes, besides the Roman Pontiff, all who rule or govern a diocese or an ecclesiastical territory equivalent to a diocese: residential bishops, abbots and prelates who rule and govern autonomous ecclesiastical districts, and their vicars general; also apostolic administrators, vicars and prefects apostolic; and the vicars capitular (administrators in the United States) during the vacancy of a see, if they are such under the common law or according to approved constitutions.

With regard to the question of the division of parishes it now has to be established who among these local ordinaries has the right to effect that division. There is no problem concerning the right of residential bishops, when all points of law are observed, to act in this matter. The law is clear.[10] By the same token competence is denied the vicar general unless he has a special authorization from his bishop.[10a] The competence of vicars and prefects apostolic likewise presents no difficulty, since they have jurisdiction in this matter equal to that of residential bishops, as do abbots and prelates *nullius* for their autonomous districts,[11] since their

[7] C. 3, X, *de ecclesiis aedificandis vel reparandis*, III, 48.

[8] Sess. XXI, *de ref.*, c. 4. A later chapter will treat the division of religious parishes. Cf. also Bouix, *Tractatus de Parocho* (3. ed., Parisiis, 1880), 248, 279 (hereafter cited *De Parocho*).

[9] Canons 1427 and 1428.

[10] Canon 1427, § 1: "Possunt etiam Ordinarii ex iusta et canonica causa paroecias quaslibet, invitis quoque earum rectoribus et sine populi consensu, dividere, vicariam perpetuam vel novam paroeciam erigentes, aut earum territorium dismembrare."

[10a] Canon 1414, § 3: "Attamen Vicarii Generales nequeunt beneficia erigere nisi ex peculiari mandato."

[11] Canons 216, 2; 294. S.C. Prop. Fide, instr. 25 iul. 1920, n. 1—*AAS*, XII (1920), 331; S.C. Prop. Fide, decr. 9 dec. 1920, n. 1—*AAS*, XIII (1921), 17; Beste, *Introductio in Codicem*, p. 216; Ayrinhac, *Constitution of the Church in the New Code of Canon Law* (New York: Benziger, 1925), p. 21.

obligations to foster those things which pertain to the care of souls postulates this power. Canon 198 does not concede to vicars and prefects apostolic the right to appoint vicars general, but a decree issued shortly after the appearance of the Code gave them the right to designate a vicar delegate, who was to have "in practice all the jurisdiction in spiritual and temporal matters which the Code gives to vicars general in dioceses."[12] Hence the vicar delegate, following the law regarding vicars general, could divide parishes if he were equipped with the special mandate of the respective vicar or prefect apostolic.

Less clear, however, and basically of great importance, is the question of the competence of the cathedral chapter and of vicars capitular or administrators in this matter. It is certain that no law in the Code forbids them to erect a parish. But conflicting opinions among the authors who discuss the problem are of small assistance when an attempt is made to determine whether or not vicars capitular or administrators are competent to divide parishes.[13] Vermeersch-Creusen (1858-1936)[14] deny the power of the vicar to divide parishes in view of the analogy deducible from canon 1423, which denies to him the power to unite parishes. Ayrinhac (1867-1930)[15] and Augustine (1872-1943)[16] concur with this opinion. Augustine and Berutti[17] depart from the usual interpretation of canon 436, "*Sede vacante nihil innovetur,*" in order to strengthen their case against the competence of the vicar capitular. Coronata follows the interpretation given by the older commentators, teaching that nothing is to be done by the temporary ruler of a vacant diocese which would in any way harm or endanger the

---

[12] Bouscaren, *The Canon Law Digest* (2 vols., Milwaukee: Bruce Publishing Co., 1934-1943), I, 144; S.C. Prop. Fide, 8 dec. 1919—*AAS,* XII (1920), 120; Canon 386.

[13] In the United States, where there are no cathedral chapters, diocesan consultors elect an administrator who is equivalent in law to a vicar capitular.

[14] Epitome, II, 523 and 533.

[15] *Administrative Legislation in the New Code of Canon Law* (New York: Longmans, Green, 1930), p. 325 (hereafter cited *Administrative Legislation*).

[16] *The Canonical and Civil Status of Catholic Parishes in the United States* (St. Louis, 1926), p. 157.

[17] *Institutiones Iuris Canonici* (6 vols., Romae: Marietti, 1943), II, 169.

diocese or the episcopal rights.[18] Consequently changes or innovations which, far from endangering the diocese or offering prejudice to episcopal rights, rather are useful and enhance the status of the diocese, or also the potential capacity of the future bishop to care for souls, are not prohibited.[19]

Urging the text of canon 6, § 2, against Augustine and Berutti, one can state that their objections to the inclusions of vicars capitular as ordinaries in the matter of the dividing of parishes has no foundation in their precise manner of interpreting the canon concerned. As far as canon 436 is concerned, then, the vicar capitular, when all legal prescriptions are verified and definite beneficial effects are foreseen, can divide a parish. Coronata elsewhere states that vicars capitular, when they are not excluded in the law, are to be considered ordinaries when the erection of benefices is concerned.[20] Sipos agrees,[21] and Cappello likewise urges that vicars capitular be considered competent in this matter.[22]

Connolly suggests that an objection could be raised relative to the power of the vicar capitular on the grounds that he cannot confer a parish until a year after the diocese has become vacant.[23] Since the difficulty would pass at the end of the year, or be supplied through a parochial administrator, the objection carries little weight.

In support of Coronata and Cappello an argument suggests itself. Recent years have demonstrated that great calamities, such as World War II, can cause rapid fluctuations in population, large scale migrations, and a general dislocation of established parishes. The situation could arise, in such circumstances, when the need for a new parish would become so serious as to brook no delay. Certainly the spirit of the law tends to supply for the silence, and it seems that the vicar capitular could then divide a

[18] *Institutiones Iuris Canonici,* I, 555; Reiffenstuel, lib. III, tit. 9, n. 16; Schmalzgrueber, lib. III, tit. 9, n. 28.

[19] *Loc. cit.*

[20] *Op. cit.,* II, n. 977, footnote, n. 3.

[21] *Enchiridion Iuris Canonici* (4. ed., Pécs. ex Typographia "Haladás R.T.," 1940), p. 728.

[22] *Summa Iuris Canonici,* II, n. 537.

[23] *The Canonical Erection of Parishes,* p. 49; cf. canon 455, § 2, 3°.

parish. "Those in charge of the administration [of a diocese] are fully entitled to better the condition of the diocese in any manner they see fit,"[24] and, in the case at hand, when no measures but the erection of a parish by division could best supply the needs of the people concerned, the diocese would benefit immeasurably by the action of the vicar capitular.

Although the competence of the vicar capitular to divide parishes is denied by some authors, there is sufficient support in favor of his authority to conclude that in given circumstances, at least, the division of a parish by a vicar capitular would be upheld by the Sacred Congregation of the Council.

Permanent apostolic administrators enjoy the same powers as residential bishops to divide parishes. If they are appointed only temporarily, they follow the law prescribed for vicars capitular.[25]

---

[24] Jaeger, *The Administration of Vacant and Quasi-Vacant Dioceses in the United States,* The Catholic University of America Canon Law Studies, n. 81 (Washington, D. C.: The Catholic University of America, 1932), pp. 190-191.

[25] Canon 315, §§ 1 and 2.

CHAPTER V

Canonical Causes for the Division of Parishes

Canon 1427, § 2.—Causa canonica ut divisio aut dismembratio paroeciae fieri possit, ea tantum est, si aut magna sit difficultas accedendi ad ecclesiam paroecialem, aut nimia sit paroecianorum multitudo, quorum bono spirituali subveniri nequeat ad normam can. 476, § 1.

Canon 1428, § 2.—Unio, translatio, divisio, dismembratio facta sine canonica causa irrita est.

History has demonstrated that the Church can accomplish her divine mission most effectively through the parochial institute. Consequently, she seeks constantly to provide the faithful with all the facilities, both temporal and spiritual, necessary for the fulfillment of her purpose. Realizing that stability in parishes is fundamental to success, she has often shown extreme reluctance to disturb the status of any parish until all other means needed for this purpose have been utilized.[1] The Council of Trent commanded that no change was to be enforced in a parish so long as through the addition of assistant priests there could be provided the necessary care of souls.[2] This conception of stability in parishes may be traced ultimately to the old practice of discouraging all forms of alienation without sufficient cause.[3]

The division of benefices, particularly of parochial benefices, has always been considered something disagreeable since it deprives the beneficiary or the pastor of certain temporal and spiritual rights. Division implies not only the removal of part of the

[1] Council of Toulouse (843 or 844), c. 7—*MGH, Leges,* I, 279; Hardouin, IV, 1459.

[2] Sess. XXI, *de ref.*, c. 4.

[3] Abbas Panormitanus (Nicholaus de Tudeschis, 1386-1453) stated: "Non enim debet sine causa parochialis ecclesia dividi. Est enim ista alienatio iurium ecclesiae quae sine causa fieri non debet."—*Lectura in Lib. III Decretalium,* cap. 3, tit. 48, n. 2.

territory of a parish and the consequent loss of jurisdiction to the pastor, but also the loss of revenue from the faithful living within that territory. In the United States, where most parishes depend upon voluntary contributions for their support, the division of a parish could involve serious decline in revenue, and eventually a serious interference with the proper care of souls, unless the law would safeguard the spiritual and temporal rights of the pastor and the parish.

The present law takes into account the ancient concept of stability in parishes. It not only declares that certain causes must be present before ordinaries can divide parishes, but also clearly asserts the causes themselves. Furthermore, the reluctance of the Church to deprive beneficiaries of acquired rights is demonstrated by the nullifying clause of canon 1428, § 2, namely, that one or the other of the two canonical causes must be present before a valid division can occur. Traditionally the status of the Church can be changed only when a justifying cause exists, and ordinarily all just causes can be reduced to this, that without change, and in this case without division, the obligations annexed to the parochial office cannot be satisfied.[4]

Before any analysis of the canonical causes in detail, it seems necessary to ascertain precisely when validity of the causes would not be admissible. The Code rules that in preference to the division of a parish the spiritual good of the people should first be consulted through the placing of assistants (*vicarii cooperatores*) in the parish.[5] This law had its inception in the Council of Trent,[6] which continued the earlier legislation that made the dividing of a parish an extraordinary remedy for the spiritual ills of a parish.[7]

The Code does not renew the prescriptions of the earlier law concerning the avoidance of division by appointing curates in dependent chapels located within the parish boundaries in order to obviate the causes for a division and properly to supply the needs

---

[4] Schmalzgrueber, lib. III, tit. 48, n. 7. Cf. S.C.C., *Causa Verulana,* 22 maii 1784—*Thesaurus,* LII, 117 and 123; Bouix, *De Parocho,* pp. 253 ff.

[5] Canon 476, 1; 1427, § 2.

[6] Sess. XXI, *de ref.,* c. 4.

[7] Council of Tours (1163)—c. 8, X, *de praebendis et dignitatibus,* III, 5. Cf. Panormitanus, Lib. III, tit. 48, n. 8.

of the faithful. But the spiritual welfare of the people is the chief concern of the new law,[8] and it is left to the prudence of the ordinary to determine whether the appointment of additional priests or the dividing of the parish can best serve the interests of his people. The ordinary, in determining the most effective procedure, can be expected either to be familiar or to familiarize himself with the particular circumstances peculiar to the parish concerned, in order to ascertain the action called for. Consequently his judgment is sanctioned in law, since on him rests the chief burden of the care of souls in his diocese, and to him is pre-eminently applied the old axiom: *Salus animarum suprema lex est.*[9]

In larger parishes, where the territory is scattered, and the number of the faithful great, a division of the parish seems to have the stronger support in law. For the mere addition of curates to the parish could hardly overcome the difficulties of distance and numbers. In localities where it is customary for curates to live apart from the pastor, but within the parish, and to be in charge of succursal chapels or missions, the need for a division would surely be less pronounced. However satisfactory such a system might prove, it hardly conforms to the command of the Council of Trent and the present law that pastors know their sheep.[10] Nor does it agree with the late nineteenth century jurisprudence of the Sacred Congregation of the Council which insisted that the Church gives the pastor to the people, not the people to the pastor.[11] The Code itself urges a community life for the parish priest where this can be done prudently.[12] Consequently, when there is some

---

[8] Canon 476, § 8. "Si nec per vicarios cooperatores spirituali fidelium bono consuli rite queat, Episcopus provideat ad normam can. 1427."

[9] Beste, *Introductio in Codicem,* p. 704; De Meester, *Juris Canonici et Juris Canonico-Civilis Compendium* (nova ed., 3 vols. in 4, Brugis: Desclée, De Brouwer, 1921-1928), Vol. III, pars I, 410 (hereafter cited *Compendium*).

[10] Sess. XXIII, *de ref.,* c. 1; canon 467, § 1.

[11] S.C.C., *Ianuen., Dismembrationis,* 25 ian. 1879—*Thesaurus,* CXXXVIII (1879), 56-65.

[12] Canon 476, § 5, and canon 134. Cf. Beste, *Introductio in Codicem,* p. 186; Augustine, *A Commentary on the New Code of Canon Law* (3. ed., 8 vols., St. Louis: Herder, 1919-1931), II, 575 (hereafter cited *A Commentary on Canon Law*).

question regarding the most efficient method of providing a particular parish with the proper pastoral care, ordinaries must seek the solution by means of a careful consideration of the particular circumstances in the parish concerned and by examining the arguments in favor of each position. The utility and necessity of the Church, which really are the fundamental reasons for the change to be effected, should be the first concern, with the law serving as the guide for the prudent resolution of the problem.[13]

A second possibility regarding the non-admissibility of the canonical causes suggests itself. Oftentimes it will happen that parishes have boundaries which are no longer equitable, and in consequence occasion inconveniences, because of the distance involved, to the people who live on the outer edges of the parish. At the same time another parish church may be much closer to them than the one to which they are subject. It is only natural that many such people will seek out the closer church. Contact with their legal pastor is lost, and it becomes well-nigh impossible for the pastor to fulfill his obligations towards them.

Theoretically indeed a cause for division may be present, and perhaps the other requirements of law can also be verified in the case. But the problem could in reality be better solved by means of a dismemberment. Dismemberment is defined as the withdrawal of a part of the territory or of goods of a benefice and the assignment of it to another benefice or to a charitable or other ecclesiastical institute.[14] In the dismemberment of a parish the same causes are stated in the law as for a division.[15] Many others taught that a dismemberment in the strict sense was verified only when part of the revenue of a benefice was separated and applied to another.[16] Canon 1427, § 1, permits the separation of part of the territory and the segregation of a proportionate part of the revenue, if any, and the application of both to the other parish. Coronata observes that it is not necessary when a territory is dis-

---

[13] Rossi, *De Paroecia* (Romae: Pustet, 1923), p. 26.

[14] Canon 1421.

[15] Canon 1427, § 1.

[16] Reiffenstuel, lib., III, tit. 12, n. 24; Wernz, *Jus Decretalium*, II, n. 269; Ojetti, *Synopsis Rerum Moralium et Iuris Pontificii* (Romae, 1899), s.v. *Dismembratio*.

membered that the revenue or the endowment be also dismembered.[17] Circumstances will properly determine in a given case when the revenue of the church from which some territory and people are to be withdrawn must also be dismembered.[18]

Territorial dismemberment, then, can serve as an appropriate remedy for the undesirable consequences of boundaries no longer satisfactory. Also through the parochial re-assignment of souls inadequately cared for or put to grave inconvenience as a result of population changes over a period of years, Ordinaries can abstract from the need of dividing a parish and thus cancel out the subsequent increased financial burden that the erection of a new parish would entail. If it is foreseen that a dismemberment will provide only a temporary measure of relief, then the ordinary would do well to use the powers granted him by law to procure the best protection for souls by erecting a new parish through a division of the older parish.

Dismemberment could be favored as the best means of settling a difficulty when the very shortage of priests in the diocese forestalls all chances for an adequate staffing of a new parish. A rearrangement of boundaries could shift some of the burdens to other priests, thereby establishing a more balanced allotment in the performance of imperative parochial obligations.

Ultimately it is left to the judgment of the ordinary to determine when the causes stated in canon 1427, § 2, will prompt a dismemberment or a division, since it is for him to seek out the most efficient means of providing for the faithful in his diocese.[19]

Concerning the inadmissibility of canonical causes for the division of parishes the conclusion is obvious that in the last analysis the ordinary must decide whether the circumstances in a particular parish demand a solution which looks to the addition of curates, to dismemberment, to a division, as the best calculated means for serving the interests of souls. The law states the causes for which the alternatives of dismemberment or of division may be applied,

---

[17] *Institutiones Iuris Canonici,* II, p. 376, footnote n. 6.

[18] De Meester, *Compendium,* vol. III, pars I, n. 1410, p. 334; Cappello, *Summa Iuris Canonici,* II, 521. Cf. S.C.C., *Utinen.,* 14 ian. 1922—*AAS,* XIV (1922), 229.

[19] *De Paroecia,* p. 26.

but the decision regarding which of these is to be invoked in particular cases rests with the chief shepherd of the diocese. The analysis of the canonical causes which follows herewith should be of great assistance in determining the application of the law in cases wherein the issue is somewhat unclear in the dim light of the attending circumstances.

ARTICLE 1. GREAT DIFFICULTY FOR PARISHIONERS TO ATTEND THE PARISH CHURCH

First named of the two causes demanded by canon 1427, § 2, for the division of parishes is that of the great difficulty for parishioners to attend the parish church. Such a difficulty can be twofold, arising either from the factor of the distance which separates them from the church or from the consideration of the hardship experienced by them in reaching the church in the light of the various obstacles that have intervened.[20] The law concerning the difficulty of approach to the church as a canonical cause has been the same since the Council of Trent,[21] but the interpretation of the law has suffered many substantial changes, as the mellowing influence of altered circumstances changed the view of the Rota and of the Sacred Congregation of the Council. According to the Council of Trent the one general cause for which a division was allowed was the grave inconvenience (*magnum incommodum*) which the faithful experienced in reaching the church. Even when such an inconvenience was obvious, but the needs of the people could be met by means of the appointment of extra curates or the establishing of priests in dependent chapels, division was forbidden.

Commentators on the pre-Code law insisted that distance and difficulty of approach were not in themselves sufficient causes for the effecting of a division. Either or both had to be present in such a manner as to give rise to a grave inconvenience.[22] Otherwise a just cause for division did not exist. The law left it to the judg-

---

[20] Bouix, *De Parocho*, p. 252.

[21] Sess. XXI, *de ref.*, c. 4.

[22] Bouix, *De Parocho*, p. 257; Leurenius, *Forum Beneficiale* (2 vols., Venetiis, 1742), II, q. 154.

ment of the ordinary to determine whether the factor of inconvenience was grave enough to warrant a division as the only means of resolving the problem.

Authors mentioned some reasons which the bishop could contemplate when he sought to avail himself of the best method of protecting his people. Reasons justifying a division on the basis of difficulty of approach were such as the following: the impassability of the roads at certain times during the year, especially during winter, the absence of bridges over rivers or streams, the perils which attend the necessary traversing of swamplands, the hazards of roving wild animals, the danger in negotiating precipitous paths, and other similar natural hindrances.[23] The suggested reasons indicated a rigid interpretation of the law, and most of them would not frequently be encountered in modern times. Present-day bishops can substitute as reasons analagous to the older difficulties today's express highways, grade crossings, and well-travelled thoroughfares, particularly where there are many children, as well as bad country roads, which often become quagmires in inclement weather. Also adequate reasons can be deduced from such circumstances as the remoteness of the church from public transportation lines, or from the mere fact that many parishioners must use some form of public transportation to reach the church. The latter is a sufficient reason in itself for a division, since "many people, even in prosperous times, cannot afford to travel by public or private conveyance without great hardship."[24]

Difficulty of approach due to natural obstacles as a cause for division was the source of many appeals to the Rota and the Sacred Congregation of the Council. The decisions of the tribunals betray a gradual tendency to relax the rigid interpretations of the Tridentine law, which enjoyed popularity until the eighteenth century.[25] Previous Rota decisions had consistently refused to

---

[23] Ferraris, *Bibliotheca,* s.v. *Dismembratio,* n. 14; Rossi, *De Poroecia,* p. 26.

[24] Connolly, *The Canonical Erection of Parishes,* p. 55.

[25] S.R.R., *Oveten.,* 12 maii 1681—*Decisiones,* 578, part. 19, tome II, *recent.,* n. 8, p. 470. "Domini, praesupposita etiam subsistentia causarum, eas non sufficere crediderunt quotiescumque potest aliunde provideri, cum dismembratio sit remedium extraordinarium et subsidiarium, ad quod numquam a Iudicibus devenire solet, quotiescumque adsit aliud remedium minus odiosum,

permit division save as an extreme remedy.[26] Fagnanus (1598-1678), a commentator of this period, and a secretary of the Sacred Congregation of the Council,[27] favored a less strict interpretation of the reason based on the difficulty of approach to the church demanding as a justifying reason for division only a relative impossibility for the parishioners to attend divine services.[28]

In the middle of the eighteenth century economic, social, and religious conditions seemed to influence the Sacred Congregation of the Council toward a more liberal interpretation of the law. One decision,[29] for example, clearly indicated the trend to a milder view of the reason "great inconvenience" demanded in the Council. A century later the Sacred Congregation stated that the supreme law in matters pertaining to the causes for division is the salvation of souls, since for that purpose pastors are given to the people. The case prompting this statement was one that involved a parish which had overcome satisfactorily the obstacle of difficulty of approach by the placing of curates in outlying chapels. Arguments against the decree of the bishop who had divided the parish were held to be less telling than those proposed in favor of his judgment. Hardships of travel and the distance from the parish church made it necessary for many to attend the chapels exclusively, de-

---

et exorbitans."—Cf. S.R.R., *Leodien. Dismembrationis,* 1 febr. 1712, *coram Falconerio,* Dec. XXXIV, IV, p. 79; also S.C.C., *Lunen. Sarazen., Dismembrationis paroeciae,* 27 sept. 1732—*Thesaurus,* V (1730), 376. S.C.C. (*Cassanen.,* 17 dec. 1740) voided a division which could have been prevented by means of the appointment of curates—*Thesaurus,* IX (1739-1740), 101, secundo.

[26] S.R.R., *Comen.,* 22 iun. 1648 *Coram Corrado*—referred to by Bouix, *De Parocho,* p. 260.

[27] Van Hove, *Prolegomena ad Codicem Iuris Canonici* (ed. altera, Mechliniae et Romae: Dessain, 1945), p. 537.

[28] *Commentaria super Quinque Libros,* Lib. III, tit. 48, c. 3, n. 2.

[29] "Censuit enim deveniendum esse ad dismembrationem paroeciae, tametsi rector veteris parochiae retinere offeret in aliqua cappella capellanum qui occurrere valeret spiritualibus indigentiis parochianorumm qui iusta de causa instabant pro dismembratione."—S.C.C., *Comen.,* 3 dec. 1750—cited in S.R.R., *Lucana,* 23 apr. 1917—*AAS,* IX, 1917), 511. See also S.C.C., *Reatina,* 20 sept. 1817—*Thesaurus,* LXXVII (1817), 286.

priving many parishioners of even a remote contact with their pastor. This last was particularly true of the very aged and the children—those most in need of pastoral ministrations.[80]

In the remarks which follow the decision the consultor indicated that a division was no longer an extreme remedy in the juridical practice of the time, if the good of souls was cultivated through the procedure, and a sufficient revenue for the support of both parishes was assured. A practical observation was made to the effect that it was the policy of the Congregation to support the act of a bishop dividing a parish, even when certain formalities had been omitted. This opinion coincided with that expressed in an earlier decision.[81]

The older practice of serving the people by means of succursal chapels was impugned by the Sacred Congregation of the Council at a later date as not conforming with the law of the Council of Trent that "distincto populo incertas propriasque parochias suum perpetuum peculiaremque parochum assignent, qui eas cognoscere valeat, et a quo solo licite sacramenta recipiant."[82] The consultor in this last case asserted that the necessity and the utility of the Church constituted the general causes for division. These causes were verified as often as parishioners were unable to go to the parish church to receive the sacraments or to assist at divine services. He further adverted to the decree of the Council of Trent that pastors were required to know their "sheep," feed them by preaching the word of God, administer the sacraments to them, and otherwise by their example manifesting everything good.[83] Other reasons which the same consultor held to be sufficient for the division of a parish, according to the constant practice of the

---

[80] S.C.C., *Scarmagno,* 29 sept. 1879—*ASS,* XIII (1880), 279. Cf. Rucupis, "The Canonical Formation of Parishes and Missions," *The Ecclesiastical Review,* LV (1916), 238-250 (*American Ecclesiastical Review*—1889-1905; *The Ecclesiastical Review,* 1905-1943; *American Ecclesiastical Review*—1944-).

[81] Cf. *AAS,* XIII (1880), 307.

[82] Sess. XXIV, *de ref.,* c. 13, referred to in S.C.C., *Concordien.,* 19 ian. 1889—*ASS,* XXII (1889), 74.

[83] Sess. XXIII, *de ref.,* c. 1.

Congregation, were antipathies, rivalries (*simultates*), and hatred among factions or towns of the same parish.[34]

Shortly before the publication of the Code the jurisprudence of the Rota revealed a trend even more liberal. In deciding a case it observed "that nowadays dismemberment (division) is to be made more easily, and is no longer to be considered, as it was formerly, an extreme remedy not to be applied when the care of souls could be provided for otherwise, for instance, by means of a vicar. The reason for this milder practice is that today the lax morals of youth and the devestating inroads of masonic sects, which prowl about like hungry wolves seeking to devour the flock of Christ, indicate at least the evident utility, if not the absolute necessity, of multiplying shepherds. Among the shepherds everybody realizes that true pastors are to be preferred to vicars."[35]

Evident utility, the foundation of any change of status of the Church was held as the more generic source which embraced the causes which had been named by the Council of Trent, and it was the consideration of utility which was to prompt the bishop to determine whether in a given case there were present causes which warranted the act of dividing a parish.[36] In the earlier law as in the present there were no rules for determining the presence of canonical causes. That task was left to the prudence of the bishop.[37]

Laxity in the interpretation of the causes for division was suddenly halted with the publication of the Code. The present law recognizes as the sole canonical causes for division the great difficulty for parishioners to approach the parish church, or a number

---

[34] S.C.C., *Concordien.*, 19 ian. 1889—*ASS*, XXII (1889), 74. Cf. also S.R.R., *Bobien.*, 4 mart. 1911, decis. XII, n. 2—*Decisiones coram Lega*, p. 166.

[35] S.R.R., *Sedunen.*, 2 apr. 1912, Dec. XIII, n. 4—*AAS*, IV (1912), 454; *Decisiones*, IV (1912), 154 (translation by the writer). Cf. Connolly, *The Canonical Erection of Parishes*, pp. 53-54.

[36] Sebastianelli, *Praelectiones Juris Canonici, De Rebus* (Romae, 1905), p. 326.

[37] Bargilliat, *Praelectiones Juris Canonici* (36 ed., 2 vols., Parisiis, 1923), II, 58; Cocchi, *Commentarium in Codicem Iuris Canonici* (4 ed., 8 vols. in 5, Taurinorum Augustae: Marietti, Vol. I, 1931; Vol. II, 1937; Vol. III, 1937; Vol. IV, 1938; Vol. V, 1938; Vol. VI, 1942; Vol. VIII, 1938), VI, pp. 224 and 225.

of parishioners so great as to preclude proper spiritual care by the pastor with the aid of assistants. No longer can such reasons as dissensions among the people, or simple utility when it merely makes more convenient what was already not very difficult, be adduced as sufficient causes in themselves.[38]

An analysis of the words "great difficulty" is necessary for a thorough understanding of the canonical cause under discussion. How great must it be? The law uses the word *magna*, not *maxima*. It thereby implies that the difficulty does not have to be very great, and thus it leads to the conclusion that the difficulty according to the mind of the legislator is to be regarded in a relative light. As long as the difficulty proves sufficient subjectively to keep a notable number of the faithful from going to the parish church or Mass and the sacraments, it can be considered a canonical cause.[39] This conclusion receives support from the fact that the final decision in regard to the sufficiency of the difficulty as a valid cause for a division rests with the ordinary. He must evaluate the facts in a particular case and rest his judgment on them, rather than on some inflexible precedents. To aid this decision the opinion of the people in the territory is of great assistance.[40] The law itself demands consultation with the interested parties.[41]

Often those things which are considered difficult for people dwelling in cities are held to be the normal thing in rural areas.[42] Some authors are of the opinion that the difficulty of approach is verified not only on the basis of distance or of arduous traveling, but also on the basis of the church's capacity, i.e., when the parish church is too small to accommodate all the faithful.[43] However, it appears more likely that such a reason more properly justifies a division on the grounds of an excessive number of parishioners.

---

[38] Pistocchi, *De Re Beneficiali iuxta Canones* (Taurini: Marietti, 1928), p. 117 (hereafter referred to as *De Re Beneficiali*).

[39] Ayrinhac, *Administrative Legislation*, p. 326.

[40] De Luca, *Theatrum Veritatis et Iustitiae*, Tom. III, *De decimis*, p. III, disc. 12, n. 9; Connolly, *The Canonical Erection of Parishes*, p. 55.

[41] Canon 1428, § 1.

[42] Coronata, *Institutiones Iuris Canonici*, II, 379.

[43] Coronata, *loc. cit.*; Augustine, *A Commentary on Canon Law*, VI, 509 and 510.

How much distance from the parish church constitutes a source of great inconvenience? The law itself does not answer the question, but, as in the judgment regarding grave inconvenience in other matters, leaves it to the discretion of the ordinary to determine in particular cases when the factor of distance constitutes a canonical cause. That the law refrains from any declaration is logical enough, for different localities within a nation, or even within the same diocese, can have different views concerning the nature of the difficulties which distance entails. In the United States, for instance, rural communities consider a distance of eight to ten miles, more in some areas, as nothing extraordinary. On the other hand, those living in a big city are accustomed to as many as five or six churches in the same area. The ordinary must consider these opinions in preference to looking for some general norm to cover all cases.

Roman decisions on the matter offer varying answers to the question. They have referred to a one or two hours' walk, to a distance of 1500 *passus* (about a mile and a quarter), to a distance of three Italian miles, and at times simply to a long and arduous way.[44] The practice of the Roman tribunals has been to uphold the bishop's act of the division of a parish when a notable portion of the people resided two miles from the parish church, and to deny confirmation for his decree when the distance was less than one and a half miles.[45] Although a safe general rule cannot be drawn from particular decisions, it would appear generally that the distance approved by the tribunals would serve as a kind of guide for ordinaries in normal circumstances.

The great difficulty for parishioners to attend the parish church, then, is a factor which is subject to local opinions and to the judgment of the bishop. Naturally a flexible cause in view of its needed adaptability to every possible circumstance which nature and hu-

---

[44] Augustine, *A Commentary on Canon Law,* VI, 509; S.C.C., *Brixinen.,* 22 iun. 1743—*Thesaurus,* XII, 103; S.C.C., *Lunen., Sarazen.,* 27 sept. 1732—*Thesaurus,* V, 377; S.C.C., *Syracusana,* 28 mar. 1903—*Analecta Ecclesiastica* (Paris, 1893-1911), XI (1903), 116 ff.

[45] S.R.R., *Sedunen.,* 2 apr. 1912, Dec. XIII, n. 3—*Decisiones,* IV (1912), 153; S.C.C., *Placentina,* 28 maii 1791—*Thesaurus,* LX (1791), 136; S.C.C., *Aquen.,* 2 aug. 1721—*Thesaurus,* II (1721-1723), 56.

man whims can create, it remains for the chief shepherd of a diocese to settle each case as it arises according to his conscience and with the law as his guide.

ARTICLE 2. THE EXCESSIVE NUMBER OF PARISHIONERS

The second cause which canon 1427, § 2, admits to be sufficient for the division of parishes is that of an excessive number of parishioners. A restriction, however, is placed on this cause by the law. When a pastor can satisfactorily supply the spiritual needs of his people by receiving assistant priests to help him to secure the best possible service, this cause for division vanishes.[46]

Never in the pre-Code law was an excessive number of the faithful admitted as a sufficient cause in itself for the division of a parish.[47] The present law follows the Council of Trent insofar as it states that assistants are to be given to a pastor who is unable to cope with his pastoral obligations in view of the number of the faithful committed to him,[48] but it provides for the situation which arises when the appointment of assistant priests does not answer the problem created by an excessive number of faithful by permitting a division for that cause.[49] The present law, then, clarifies to a certain degree the circumstances under which this cause may be admitted as a sufficient reason for effecting the division. The ordinary is to judge under precisely what circumstances the need cannot be met through the granting of assistants to the pastor.

In order to determine as closely as possible a general, if very flexible norm in this matter, a study of recent jurisprudence is necessary. Prior to the Code, although the law itself made no mention of the excessive number of the faithful in a parish as a cause for its division, the Sacred Congregation of the Council as a matter of fact did allow divisions solely upon the evidence that the pastor and his assistants could not fulfill their obligations

---

[46] Canon 476, § 1.

[47] Fagnanus, lib. III, tit. 48, c. 3, n. 24.

[48] Canon 486, § 1; sess. XXI, *de ref.*, c. 4.

[49] Canon 476, § 8. "Si nec per vicarios cooperatores spirituali fidelium bono consuli rite queat, Episcopus provideat ad normam can. 1427."

properly in consequence of the unusually large numbers of the faithful.[50]

The reasons for this seeming departure from the law can be found in the explanation given by Bouix (1808-1870), who found it difficult to concede that the legislator approved of the existence of parishes which numbered as many as thirty thousand souls. He maintained that the cases of parishes which contained such numbers were not foreseen as possible at the time the law was put into effect.[51] Ferraris mentioned one case in which the pastor offered to erect a chapel to be staffed by a resident vicar in order to forestall the division of his parish by the bishop.[52] The Sacred Congregation of the Council approved the division of the parish despite this precautionary move. A year later the Congregation denied an appeal made by a pastor against the division of a parish in which two auxiliary chapels had been erected.[53] Later still a consultor stated bluntly that it was the practice of the Sacred Congregation of the Council to confirm and commend the division of a parish notwithstanding the presence of chapels.[54] Assurance that in fact, if not in law, an excessive number of parishioners was considered as a sufficient cause for a division is discovered in the precise statement of one consultor in the *Acta Sanctae Sedis* that such was the case.[55]

In the absence of any official universal declaration from the

---

[50] S.C.C., 5 dec. 1750—*Thesaurus,* XIV (1749-1750), 147; S.C.C., Verulana, 22 maii 1784—*Thesaurus,* LIII (1784), 117 and 123; S.C.C., *Laquedonien.,* 16 dec. 1876—*Thesaurus,* CXXXV (1876), 618; S.C.C., *Taurinen.,* 21 ian. 1905—*Thesaurus,* CLXIV (1905), 112 ff.

[51] *De Parocho,* pp. 255 and 256.

[52] *Bibliotheca,* s.v. *Dismembratio,* n. 37; S.C.C., *Comen.,* 5 dec. 1750—*Thesaurus,* XIV (1749-1750), 147.

[53] S.C.C., *Nolana,* 3 feb. 1751—cited by Ferraris, *Bibliotheca,* s.v. *Dismembratio,* n. 38.

[54] "Praxis est S.C. Concilii, quae consuevit commendare et confirmare dismembrationem et paroeciae erectionem . . . , non obstante oblatione facta providendi per cappellanum."—S.C.C., *Laquedonien.,* 16 dec. 1876—*Thesaurus,* CXXXV (1876), 618; *Analecta Ecclesiastica,* XIII (1903), 27.

[55] "Auctum nimis populi numerum, et distantiam a Parochiali Ecclesia, praecipuas esse ex iure canonum causas dismembrationis concedendae."—*ASS,* XII (1879), 293.

Holy See as establishing the maximum population allowed in a parish, a general norm may be sought in the practical disposition of some cases made by the Sacred Congregation of the Council. Official pronouncements are widely divergent, as Connolly[56] remarks, but some authors find in these pronouncements an indication, at least, of certain limits beyond which the proper parochial work is difficult to achieve.[57] Pius VI (1775-1799), in writing to the bishops of France (March 10, 1791), strongly disapproved of the practice of having as many as six thousand parishioners in one parish in Paris. In his writing the Pope contended that such a number "longe longeque unius parochi vires excedet."[58] There was no mention of assistants in this document, and consequently the text seemed to reflect the mind of the Pope for all cases, even if assistants were stationed at the parish. Bouix indicated his mind on the subject when he asked the question, "What would Pope Pius VI have to say concerning present-day late nineteenth century parishes in Paris which embrace 30,000 or more souls?"[59] Could not the same question be asked concerning some of the larger parishes in our metropolitan cities?

In the face of so strong a precedent, the Sacred Congregation of the Council weighed thoroughly the recourse of a pastor against the decree of his bishop who had divided his parish for the sole reason that it cared for as many as 32,000 souls! Fifteen curates had been assigned the pastor, and it was his contention that the faithful were receiving adequate service. The Congregation sustained the decree of the bishop.[60]

Further illustrating the issue is another case in which the action of a bishop who had divided a parish under the care of the

---

[56] *The Canonical Erection of Parishes*, p. 57.

[57] Bouix, *De Parocho*, p. 256; Coronata, *Institutiones Iuris Canonici*, II, 379; De Meester, *Compendium*, Vol. III, pars I, 334; Ayrinhac, *Administrative Legislation*, pp. 326 and 327.

[58] Const. "Quod aliquantum"—cited by Bouix, *De Parocho*, p. 256. This constitution is not traceable to the *Fontes* or the Bullaria. Ayrinhac refers to it in his *Administrative Legislation*, p. 326, under the title *Aliquantulum.*

[59] *De Parocho*, p. 257.

[60] S.C.C., *Syracusana*, 28 mart. 1903—*Fontes*, n. 4313.

Capuchins was at the time deemed unwise. The bishop had considered 6,500 souls excessive. Two years later, however, when the population had increased further, the division was confirmed.[61] A Rota decision sometime later approved the division of a mission in Canada, where the chief reason expressed was the fact that there were four thousand parishioners. Other reasons were alleged also, but apparently the number concerned and their position in the town were of prime concern to the bishop.[62] The decision referred to a ruling incorporated in the Provincial Council of Westminster (1852), according to which there had been acknowledged to bishops the right to erect parishes whenever the necessity or utility of the faithful required it.[63]

Modern authors maintain that a parish of six thousand souls is too large, and consequently should be divided.[64] In the new division and dismemberment of parishes in Rome, Pope Leo XIII assigned no more than 3,000 souls to each.[65] The reason behind this move appears to be founded on two truths, namely, that bishops have been given special powers by the law to determine what they deem the most effective measures in accomplishing their work, and secondly that ecclesiastical jurisprudence, manifested in numerous decisions of the Roman tribunals, has indicated an awareness of the necessity of dividing parishes, lest they become too large to allow for an effective care of souls. Spiritual progress is the thing most sought after in divisions approved by these decisions. It can be said that as long as sufficient support is present or prudently foreseen, the Sacred Congregation of the Council approves the division of large parishes. The mind of the two Popes has been given, and consequently there is some support, at least, for the

---

[61] S.C.C., *Taurinen.*, 21 ian. 1905; 27 iul. 1907—*Fontes,* nn. 4320; 4339; *Thesaurus,* CLXIV (1905), 112 ff.

[62] *Causa Londonen.*, 5 aug. 1914—*AAS,* VII (1915), 73-83.

[63] ". . . licebit episcopo . . . novas ecclesias condere, ac portionem districtus iis attribuere, si necessitas aut utilitas populi fidelis id requirat."—Dec. XIII, n. 6.

[64] Coronata, *Institutiones Iuris Canonici.* III, 983; De Meester, *Compendium,* III, pars I, p. 334.

[65] De Meester, *Compendium,* III, pars I, p. 334, footnote n. 4.

opinion of authors that a compact parish with a relatively small number of parishioners makes for the better care of souls.[66]

Strong opposition to a liberal interpretation and application of the rule based on the excessive number of parishioners as a cause for division is voiced by Rossi, who insists that it would be fruitless to adduce as a cause for division the incapacity of a parish church to accommodate all the parishioners. He urges instead an enlarging of the church or the erecting of subsidiary churches or chapels, basing his interpretation on the rigid concept of division as found among the earlier commentators on the law as given by the Council of Trent.[67] Holding division to be a *res odiosa,* he reverts to the old idea of foregoing it as a general practice.[68] This concept agrees neither with the mind of the Holy See[69] nor with the expressed opinions of many authors.[70] For parishes have a special character that distinguishes them from all other benefices, inasmuch as their chief purpose is the salvation of souls. Formerly, when benefices meant a permanent endowment yielding a steady income, division appeared to be a distasteful measure to be applied only as a last resort. Today this is no longer true. The law is concerned primarily with the more efficient care of souls, and less with the beneficial character of the parish, and thus desires that the private good should cede more readily to the public welfare.

An aid to bishops in their judgment concerning an actual case in which the existence of numerous parishioners in a parish was causing some difficulty in the matter of the proper pastoral care can be evinced in a brief survey of the law concerning the obliga-

---

[66] Ayrinhac, *Administrative Legislation,* p. 327; De Meester, *Compendium,* III, pars I, 334; Coronata, *Institutiones Iuris Canonici,* 11, 983; Woywod, *A Practical Commentary on the Code of Canon Law* (2 vols., ninth printing as edited by C. S. Smith, New York: Wagner; London: Herder, 1945, II, 145 (hereafter cited *A Practical Commentary*).

[67] Fagnanus, Lib. III, tit. 48, c. 3, n. 24.

[68] Cf. S.C.C., *Laquedonien.,* 16 dec. 1876—*Thesaurus,* CXXXV (1876), 618; S.R.R., *Londonen.,* 5 aug. 1914—*AAS,* VII (1915), 73-83.

[69] *De Paroecia,* p. 28.

[70] Ayrinhac, *Administrative Legislation,* p. 327; De Meester, *Compendium,* III, pars I, 334; Woywod, *A Practical Commentary,* II, 145; Coronata, *Institutiones Iuris Canonici,* II, 983.

tions of pastors. Can a pastor, in the case of so numerous a flock, comply fully with all the prescriptions of the Code concerning him? If not there is cause for division, since the obligations of a pastor stem from the rights of the faithful to his services, and he has a right to his office only in virtue of their need.

Canon 1344 imposes the obligation of preaching on the pastor, and of furnishing a homily as indicated in the law. This duty is to be performed during the Mass best attended on Sundays and holy days of obligation. He cannot habitually satisfy this obligation through another without a just cause approved by the ordinary.[71] Such causes would be chronic ill-health, complete inability to preach, and similar reasons.[72] In some very large parishes in the United States it has become impossible to fulfill this obligation, simply because it is necessary to celebrate Mass so often on days of obligation, sometimes every half hour, that there is no time for preaching. Yet the gravity of the obligation is such that the Church indicates severe penalties for grave delinquencies.[73]

The faithful, in turn, have an obligation to inform themselves in matters of faith and morals, an obligation fulfilled according to custom by means of the Sunday sermon in the parish church. Hence, there is a double burden on the pastor. The moral impossibility to preach in view of existing circumstances may constitute an excusing cause for a time, but there is the obligation of removing, if possible, the obstacle to preaching and teaching. Evidently the only solution of any practical value in the given case would be a division of the parish concerned. The situation oftentimes cannot be remedied because of the lack of available property on which to construct the new church, but when it is possible to provide a new church, there is a serious obligation to divide the parish.

Catechetical instruction for adults and children is also an obligation for the pastor.[74] True, this obligation is not a personal one,[75] but inasmuch as the obligation of catechizing adults on

---

[71] Canon 1344, § 2.

[72] Beste, *Introductio in Codicem*, p. 656; Fanfani, *De Iure Parochorum*, p. 229.

[73] Canon 2382 and canons 2182-2185.

[74] Canons 1330 and 1332.

[75] Fanfani, *De Iure Parochorum*, p. 336.

Sundays and holy days cannot in some cases be discharged for the same reasons that preaching is omitted, the faithful are denied their right to a sufficient knowledge of the eternal truths. The division of a parish would be more than merely permitted in such circumstances—it would almost be mandatory. It is absurd to find the faithful in a sceptical and heretical world ill-equipped at best to defend their most precious gift of faith because of insufficient instruction or none at all, when a division of the parish could solve the problem and relieve the pastor, and the bishop, of overwhelming burdens.[76]

When there is a parish school the obligation to instruct children, and to prepare them for the reception of the sacraments,[77] can be fulfilled more easily if the parishioners are not excessively numerous. Sunday school and other means of providing instruction must be supplied when the parish school cannot accommodate all the children, or when there is no school.[78]

The obligation of the pastor to know his "sheep," to correct them when necessary, to render assistance to the poor, and to visit the sick,[79] implies the opportunity to do so. Whenever a parish has grown beyond the capacity of a pastor, even though he has assistance, adequately to fulfill these obligations, it seems that in reality there is present an excessive number of parishioners.

Pastors, if they are to care for their flock, as the name itself implies, must exercise more than a supervisory ministry, particularly when the supervision is concerned chiefly with their assistants. In parishes with overlarge numbers of the faithful, the administrative work alone absorbs most of the pastor's time, hardly allowing him to fulfill his more important obligations.

The decision as to the presence of an excessive number of parishioners in a certain parish rests, as in every question of fact regarding the causes for a division, with the bishop. An attempt has been made in the foregoing to appraise the cause in the light of the older decisions and of the law concerning the obli-

---

[76] Cf. Beste, *Introductio in Codicem,* p. 649.

[77] Canons 1330; 854, § 5; and 787.

[78] Woywod, *A Practical Commentary,* II, 99-100; Coronata, *Institutiones Iuris Canonici,* II, 917.

[79] Canons 467 and 468.

gations of pastors with a view to establishing certain general norms which may guide a bishop in forming a prudent judgment in the matter. The permissible inferences do not manifest any clear-cut specifically determined maximum number of people as requisite to establish the reason justifying a division, but indicate a tendency to disapprove of parishes with large populations, even when a number of assistants collaborate with the pastor in his work. Reasonable, personal care and service should be expected of a pastor, and when the number of faithful is too large to allow such care and service, then certainly cause for a division is present.

Either cause alone—no matter what the source, whether it be distance, natural or artificial obstacles, or whether it be an excessive number of people—suffices to permit a lawful division.[80] It is not necessary that both causes exist simultaneously. However, if both causes are present only partially, causing the bishop to question the sufficiency of either of the two causes singly, then the cumulative effect could, in many cases, be such as to justify division.[81] Since circumstances vary from case to case, it is ultimately the judgment of the bishop which will determine when the causes are present. The foregoing analysis of the causes should manifest how application of them was made in recent history, and thus indicate at least in a general way when the division of a parish is warranted.

ARTICLE 3. MINIMUM NUMBER OF PARISHIONERS

As a corollary to the preceding article, there seems warranted a brief discussion of the minimum number of parishioners that will suffice for a new parish constituted through its being divided from another parish. The Code is silent on the problem, literally adopting the phrase *populus determinatus*[82] from the words of the Council of Trent.[83] Modern authors are as silent as the Code concerning the subject, and consequently pre-Code practice must

---

[80] Canon 1427, § 2.

[81] Connolly, *The Canonical Erection of Parishes*, p. 58.

[82] Canon 216, § 1.

[83] Sess. XXIV, *de ref.*, c. 13; sess. XXI, *de ref.*, c. 4.

serve as the determining norm. The problem, under normal circumstances, most likely would not arise, but because the population in certain localities is sparse and widely scattered, the possibility remains that newly erected parishes would have few parishioners. It is the concern of this article to attempt to define in a general way a possible basic minimum below which a new parish resulting from division could not be permitted.

The *Decretum* of Gratian contained a canon, drawn from the XVI Council of Toledo (693), which permitted the appointment of a priest over a church which had at least ten *mancipia*.[84] It is inconceivable that the Council had reference to the term in its classical meaning—slaves.[85] Certainly the glossator attached a different significance to the word. Although his brief comment is not indisputably clear, apparently *mancipia* as used in the law of Gratian meant single persons.[86] Another gloss[87] identifies *populus* with ten persons. Fagnanus argued from this that since *populus* and *decem mancipia* are synonymous, and since *populus* means ten individuals, *decem mancipia* also means ten individuals.[88]

More generally, however, canonists interpreted *mancipia* to mean families rather than individuals. Leading to this interpretation was an early decision of the Rota, which held that three homes with fifteen persons in all, or even five homes with twenty persons, was scarcely a sufficient population for a newly erected parish.[89] It was the contention of Pyrrho (+ 1686) that in the case of an already existing parish ten persons sufficed for the continuance of the parish, but he agreed with the Rota when there

---

[84] Canon 5: ". . . Sed et hoc necessarium instituere duximus, ut plures ecclesiae uni nequaquam committantur presbytero, quia solus per totas ecclesias nec efficium valet persolvere nec rebus earum necessariam curam impendere, ea scilicet ratione praecipimus, ut ecclesia, quae, usque ad decem habuerit mancipia super se habeat sacerdotem, quae vero minus aliis coniungatur ecclesiis." Hardouin, III, 1796.

[85] Cf. Leage, *Roman Private Law* (London: Macmillan, 1932), p. 96, for classical meaning.

[86] *Glossa* ad c. 3, C.X. qu. 3, s.v. *mancipia*.

[87] *Glossa* ad c. 1, X, *de electione et electi potestate*, I, 6, s.v. *populus*.

[88] Commentaria, Lib. III, tit. 48, c. 3, n. 28.

[89] S.R.R., Florentina, 22 maii 1630—*Decisiones Recentiones*, Dec. 380, nn. 8 and 28 in *Part*. V, tom. II, p. 739.

was question of establishing a new parish through its being divided from another parish.[90] Lurenius (1646-1723), basing his opinion on the wording of Gratian and on the Rota decision, maintained that at least ten families were needed.[91]

It is most reasonable to hold that the canonists and the Rota were concerned with ten persons, not in the sense of indiscriminate human beings, but as the designation of legal persons, namely the *patresfamilias*. As the heads of families these most probably were the ones counted by canonists, and with their families formed the persons belonging to the parish. In Germany, at one time, parishes were erected in some localities where there were less than ten Catholic families, but where there were enough Protestant families to raise the total beyond the basic ten.[92] Since heretics and schismatics are subjects of the Church, doctrinally this viewpoint is defensible, but canonically the ruling seems to be concerned with actual rather than potential, Catholic families.[93]

This would be especially true in the United States where the necessary support of the pastor of the parish newly erected through division comes as a general rule from the voluntary contributions of his parishioners. Canonically, bishops are obliged to provide for the proper support of the new pastor.[94] In most parishes, the contributions from ten families, regardless of their prosperity, would hardly suffice to support a pastor, and certainly stole fees from a parish of this size would provide only a negligible support. Consequently, unless other means of support should be forthcoming, or unless the prospect of an enlargement of the parish through immigration or mass conversion exists, a division should not be made.[95] Bishops, however, could provide sufficient support for the new parish from some special diocesan fund,[96] or perhaps call upon the Church Extension Society for assistance in

---

[90] Praxis Beneficiaria (Venetiis, 1735), Lib. III, c. 5, n. 10.

[91] *Forum Beneficiale*, Vol. I, pars I, q. 160. See also Pirhing, Lib. III, tit. 29, n. 1.

[92] Schmalzgrueber, Lib. III, tit. 29, n. 7.

[93] Connolly, *The Canonical Erection of Parishes*, p. 60.

[94] Canon 1427, § 3.

[95] Rossi, *De Paroecia*, p. 21.

[96] De Meester, *Compendium*, Vol. III, Pars I, 337.

maintaining the new parish. But some provision of this sort must be made before division is attempted.[97]

The permissible minimum number of parishioners, then, must be established after a study has been made of the possibility of growth in the parish, of the available endowment for the new parish from the mother church, and of an assured financial assistance from some other sources if either or both parishes are unable to supply sufficient funds. Prudence will dictate the better policy and establish the minimum number of the faithful which canonical provisions will warrant.

It is noteworthy that most of the modern canonists hold that at least ten families are requisite for constituting a parish.[98] Cappello maintains that intrinsically even fewer than ten families would be sufficient so that with respect to the validity of the act a parish with less than ten families could be erected by way of division from an existing parish.[99] No doubt he supposes the circumstances to be ideal, so that all canonical considerations are duly fulfilled. The theory holds true so long as the establishment of the parish would have met all the requirements of law, but it is seldom that such an ideal situation can be found.

---

[97] Canon 1415, § 1. "Beneficia ne erigantur, nisi constet ea stabilem et congruam dotem habere, ex qua reditus perpetuo percipiantur ad normam can. 1410." Canon 1410 enumerates the various forms this endowment may take.

[98] Cf. Rossi, *De Paroecia*, p. 21.

[99] *Summa Iuris Canonici*, II, n. 495.

CHAPTER VI

FORMALITIES TO BE OBSERVED IN THE DIVISION OF PARISHES

Before an ordinary is permitted to proceed to the division of a parish, the fulfillment of certain formalities is prescribed by the law, formalities which have as their ultimate purpose the protection of rights and the attainment of justice. The law[1] demands that no division be undertaken until moral certainty is present that a canonical cause exists, and that a division is consequently warranted in a particular instance. Although bishops are given a free hand by the law in so far as the manner of ascertaining the necessary facts is concerned,[2] the law is clear that a definite knowledge of these facts must be previously obtained.

Canon 1428, § 2, declared that a division effected without a canonical cause is invalid, and hence makes the preliminary investigation of the situation a matter of vital importance. This investigation will be directed chiefly toward discovering the existence or the non-existence of the cause or causes for which the law permits a division.[3] This can be done either by the bishop personally or through a delegate. The latter may well be the rural dean who is familiar with the locality, with the people, and perhaps also with the potential resources of the territory concerned.[4]

Beyond establishing the presence of a canonical cause for the division of a parish there will always be other considerations worthy of study before a definite decision should be made. Sometimes obstacles will present themselves which, though a cause for a division exists, might prevent, temporarily at least, the division that is contemplated. The law anticipates these difficulties when it prescribes an objective survey of the circumstances, since the bishop is concerned only with the advantage to souls to be attained

---

[1] Canon 1428, § 1.

[2] Wernz, Jus Decretalium, II, n. 267.

[3] Wernz-Vidal, *Ius Canonicum,* II, n. 167.

[4] Leurenius, *Forum Beneficiale,* Vol. I, pars I, q. 157, n. 2.

through the establishment of a new parish. To assist him in gaining all the necessary information the law states that he must consult the cathedral chapter—the diocesan consultors in this country—and any others whose interests may be involved, particularly the rectors.[5]

The following discussion presented in this chapter will be concerned with the requisite consultation in a general way, and with the particular points to be raised in the consultation, namely the determination of boundaries, the formal decree of erection, the financing of the new parish, and the right of the pastor to recourse against the decree of the bishop. These particular headings summarize the formalities established by law for the division of parishes.

ARTICLE 1. CONSULTATION

> **Canon 1428, § 1. Locorum Ordinarii uniones, translationes, divisiones, dismembrationes beneficiorum ne faciant nisi per authenticam scripturam, auditis Capitulo cathedrali et iis, si qui sint, quorum interest, praesertim rectoribus ecclesiarum.**
>
> **Canon 1416. Ante erectionem beneficii vocentur et audiantur, si qui sint, ii quorum interest.**

The obligation imposed on an Ordinary by canon 1428, § 1, to consult his cathedral chapter or diocesan consultors had its counterpart in pre-Code jurisprudence.[6] Commentators before the Code, fully aware of the silence of the Council of Trent on this point, demanded more than a mere consultation when a division was being considered. They contended that any action involving alienation called for the consent of the chapter before the bishop could proceed.[7] And the Rota confirmed this unanimous opinion when it

---

[5] Canon 1428, § 1.

[6] S.R.R., *Sedunen.*, 2 April 1912, Dec. XIII, n. 5—*Decisiones,* IV (1912), 154.

[7] Fagnanus, Lib. III, tit. 48, c. 3, n. 51; Reiffenstuel, Lib. III, tit. 48, n. 20; Pirhing, Lib. III, tit. 48, c. 3, n. 10; Schmalzgrueber, Lib. III, tit. 48, n. 20.

held that a division executed without this consent was invalid.[8] The concept of division as a species of alienation was an ancient one.[9]

The consent of the chapter was definitely required for a valid alienation at the time of Gregory IX.[10] Apparently the consent of the chapter was required for the substantial act, that is, in so far as the division itself was concerned, and not specifically for the manner of form in which the division was to be made.[11] It is to be noted that in the United States, prior to the Code, only the advice of the consultors and of the rector of the mission needed to be obtained.[12]

Today, there is no longer any need of consent from the chapter or the consultors. The Code demands only that they be cited and heard, thus substantially derogating the earlier law, and grouping in one phrase the consultors and all other interested parties. The ordinary is bound only to seek their opinions, but the obligation to do that is clear. The advice of the consultors is to be obtained while they are gathered together at one time.[13] Ordinarily it is to be expected that the consultors will have a sufficient knowledge of the circumstances of the case to form a judgment, and consequently they will be obliged to make some inspection of the parish concerned, if they are not already familiar with its difficulties. Only then will they be able to give an honest opinion. Prudence on the part of the bishop should dictate his acceptance or rejection of the opinions of the consultors, but if all or most of them concur one way or the other, the law urges bishops not to act against their judgment without a grave reason.[14]

Retaining the older law as it was commonly interpreted, the

---

[8] "Inter has solemnitates consensus capituli certe requiritur ad substantiam seu sub poena nullitatis, nisi forte v.g., in divisione paroeciarum etiam exemptorum regularium, episcopus procedit tamquam delegatus Sedis apostolicae vel (uti gr. in Gallia) consuetudine aliud obtineat."—S.R.R., *Sedunen.*, 2 April 1912—*loc. cit.*

[9] Panormitanus, Lib. III, tit. 48, c. 3, n. 2.

[10] C. 1, X, *de his quae fiunt a praelato sine consensu capituli,* III, 10.

[11] S.R.R., *Sedunen.*, 2 April 1912—*loc. cit.*

[12] *Acta et Decreta Concilii Plenarii Baltimorensis Tertii* (Baltimorae, 1886), n. 20.

[13] Augustine, *A Commentary on Canon Law,* VI, 512.

[14] Canon 105, 1°.

Code orders consultation with all other interested parties, with special reference to the rectors of the churches. The law demands the citation and hearing of anyone whose interest is involved before a benefice can be erected.[15] A distinction must be made between those who have rights in connection with the administration of the old parish, such as the pastor or the patron, and those who have no special title to those rights, but who are concerned with the prospective division, either because of possible inconvenience or other reasons they think valid.[16]

Parishioners are included in the latter group, and justly so, for frequently their opinions can be of great value to the bishop in making his decision.[17] From them the financial condition of the faithful who would be asked to support the new church could be ascertained, the stability of the population in the projected new parish more or less determined, the possibility of serious discord in the event of a division analyzed, and the advantages and disadvantages from their point of view weighed. The consent of the parishioners is not necessary,[18] since their opinions may be biased, springing possibly from old attachments, traditional feelings, or reluctance to venture into new parish programs. Such a conference would also provide an ideal opportunity for the bishop to present his reasons for the division, thus allaying any fears and even arousing enthusiasm for the project. At all events, if the bishop feels constrained to proceed with the division even in the face of vigorous opposition by the people, he is authorized to compel them to support the church.[19]

The parishioners need not be consulted individually, but some means of ascertaining their views should be utilized. Connolly suggests that a public meeting of the people of the parish in which

---

[15] Canon 1416.

[16] Connolly, *The Canonical Erection of Parishes,* p. 65.

[17] Beste, *Introductio in Codicem,* p. 703.

[18] Canon 1427, § 1.

[19] Canon 1186 indicates that bishops should exhort the people to support the church, rather than force them to do so. The Council of Trent, sess. XXI, *de ref.*, c. 4, stated that parishioners could be compelled to contribute. See S.R.R., *Sedunen.*, 2 April 1912, Dec. XIII, n. 5—*Decisiones,* IV (1912), 155.

all could express themselves would be a practical way to obtain their opinions.[20] Resolutions summarizing the opinions of the group could then be presented to the bishop by the delegates. This would simplify the procedure and at the same time fully comply with the requirements of law.

Mentioned specifically in the law as one to be heard when a division is being considered is the pastor of the parish concerned. As in the older law,[21] the consent of the pastor to a division is not required. In the Constitution of Alexander III it was decreed that the pastor could not hinder the undertaking.[22] The Council of Trent[23] and the present law[24] both include the phrase "invitis rectoribus," indicating that an unreasonable or baseless unwillingness is meant.[25] Pastors can be said to be reasonably unwilling when there is serious doubt about the existence of the canonical cause, or about the other requirements of law, such as the existence of an assured source of revenue for the new parish. The lack of the consent of the pastor is immaterial, for it is the salvation of souls that is in question, and the private good of the pastor, however sincerely he seeks to protect his interests, must yield to the public welfare.[26]

Patrons, inasmuch as they possess rights in the parish or parishes which are the subject of the consultation, must receive the same consideration as pastors, in view of their definite interest in the future of the parishes of which they are patrons.[27] However, the bishop can act against their objections to the division, just as in the case of pastors.

---

[20] *The Canonical Erection of Parishes,* p. 65. Cf. Vermeersch-Creusen, *Epitome,* II, n. 758.

[21] Conc. Trident., sess. XXI, *de ref.,* c. 4.

[22] ". . . Si vero persona matricis ecclesiae virum idoneum praesentare distulerit, vel opus ad perfectionem deduci, et virum bonum appellationis cessante diffugio instituere non omittas."—C. 3, X, *de ecclesiis aedificandis vel reparandis,* III, 48.

[23] Sess. XXI, *de ref.,* c. 4.

[24] Canon 1427, § 1.

[25] Bouix, *De Parocho,* p. 268; Wernz-Vidal, *Jus Canonicum,* II, n. 164.

[26] Wernz-Vidal, *loc. cit.*

[27] Cf. De Meester, *Compendium,* Vol. III, pars I, n. 1410, d; Coronata, *Institutiones Iuris Canonici,* II, n. 978, 2; Schmalzgrueber, Lib. III, tit. 48, n. 18.

Historically, never has the consent of the pastor or of the faithful been required for the division of parishes. The question, however, arose among canonists as to whether the bishop was obliged to summon and consult the pastor for advice before proceeding to the division, and whether the act of division was null or rescissible in the event that this formality was omitted. Earlier opinions under the pre-Code law maintained the necessity of the citation and of the hearing for the validity of the procedure in the dividing of a parish.[28] While agreeing that the objections and suggestions of pastors could be ignored by the bishop, still there was a presumption in law that pastors, though biased, could be expected to insist on the rigorous interpretation of the canonical causes demanded at that time by raising objections based on their proximity as pastors to the people and their intimate knowledge of local conditions.[29] Omission of the citation and the hearing of the pastor was considered by the Sacred Congregation of the Council to be neglecting an essential formality which the law had provided as a means of defense against unnecessary alienation of property.[30]

Denial of a hearing to the pastor was considered to be an unjust refusal to afford him an opportunity to prove, if in the particular case proof was possible, that no canonical cause existed for a valid division. If, for example, he could demonstrate that by the assignment of assistant priests the difficulty could be eliminated then there were indications that the bishop could not proceed validly to a division.[31] The bishop, of course, was not to depend solely on the arguments of the pastor, since he was permitted to act against the will of the rector, but if adminicular proofs corroborated the statements of the pastor, the bishop was not in a position to act validly.

About fifty years before the Code, contrary to the popular opinion then current, canonists and the Rota began to favor the view that the consultation with the pastor, rather than constituting an essential part of the required formalities, was but a solemnity that touched

---

[28] Fagnanus, Lib. III, tit. 48, c. 3, n. 29; Leurenius, *Forum Beneficiale,* Vol. I, pars I, q. 157, n. 4.

[29] Pirhing, Lib. III, tit. 48, n. 11; Pyrrhus, *Praxis Beneficiaria,* Lib. III, c. 2, n. 4.

[30] S.C.C., *Nullius,* 22 September 1600—*Fontes,* n. 2335.

[31] Reiffenstuel, Lib. III, tit. 48, n. 15.

the licitness of the act and that was directed toward the promotion of a better understanding of the facts in each case and toward the forestalling of hasty ill-advised division.[32]

Although the law makes no reference to persons with claims in equity to a hearing by the bishop, it seems that there could occur cases in which certain parishioners or benefactors who live outside the parish under consideration, or who have made large contributions to special funds for the older parish, would have some right to be allowed a voice in the discussion, at least concerning the disposition of the funds for which they are largely responsible. Equity seems to call for a special consideration that takes account of their position.

Furthermore, it seems wise for bishops to consult business men who are familiar with the direction and trend that residential districts will take, or with the manner in which it is likely that industrial areas will expand. Such information would be particularly valuable when the size and capacity of the new parish church are considered, but it would also have some worth even for determining the necessity of establishing a new parish. City officials could profitably be questioned in regard to their plans for parks, recreation areas, and the like. Information of this sort seems necessary when the fixing of boundaries must be attended to. Admittedly the law does make mention of whoever needs to be called by the bishop when the proposed division remains to be decided, but information gathered from well-informed sources besides those which are specifically mentioned in the law can give immeasurable assistance to a bishop bent on the most prudent and far-seeing decision.

When the parish is vacant it is impossible to cite and hear the pastor as the law requires. The question arises whether in the case of a vacancy the bishop could proceed without the formality, since there is no pastor who could be cited. Commentators before the Code held that a division should be delayed until a new pastor has

---

[32] Connolly, *The Canonical Erection of Parishes*, p. 64; *ASS*, III (1867), 400, appendix VI. See also S.R.R., *Londonen.*, 21 August 1914—*AAS*, VII (1915), 75; S.R.R., *Sedunen.*, 2 April 1912, Dec. XIII, n. 5—*Decisiones*, IV (1912), 154; Rucupis, "The Canonical Formation of Parishes and Missions" —*The Ecclesiastical Review*, LV (1916), 245 (hereafter cited E.R.); Wernz, *Jus Decretalium*, II, n. 267.

been assigned, or that the bishop should designate a special "*defensor paroeciae*" who then could act in place of the rector and exercise his rights.[33] There is no reference to such a prescription in the present law, and indeed no prescription that governed such a situation can be found in the older law. However, indirectly a text of the Clementine decretals was used in support of the view of the older canonists.[34] A special parish defender appointed by the bishop could be of some assistance in determining the existence or the non-existence of the canonical cause, and thus perhaps lend a degree of greater objectivity to the consultation.

After the consideration of the various individuals whom the law requires to be cited and heard before a division can be effected, the question regarding the legal force of the obligation on the part of the bishop remains. The problem is this: Must the bishop cite for consultation the cathedral chapter or consultors, other interested parties, and the pastor or pastors concerned, and ask their advice under pain of nullity? Or would the neglect of the obligation leave the act of division valid and legally recognized?

The law itself clearly states that only those acts are null which are expressly or equivalently declared such by law.[35] Canon 1428, § 1, uses the expression *audito Capitulo cathedrali* in referring to the prescription that the bishop must hear the suggestions of the chapter or consultors when a division is contemplated. Canon 105, 1 °, states that, when the words *audito Capitulo* are used in a law, a superior is bound to hear those persons in order to act validly. If the law alone is considered, it appears that the obligation of the bishop is such that he cannot proceed to the division of a parish without first allowing his consultors to voice their opinions. The same thing can be said for his obligation to hear the pastor.[36]

Among the commentators, however, there is a wide difference of opinion as to the effect of the omission of consultation, with the chief bone of contention the purpose of canon 105, 1°. Some authors

---

[33] Bouix, *De Parocho,* p. 268; Leurenius, *Forum Beneficiale,* Vol. I, pars I, q. 157, n. 4.

[34] C. 2, *de rebus ecclesiae non aliendis,* III, c. 4, in Clem.

[35] Canons 11 and 1680.

[36] Canon 105, 1°, includes the word *parochus* among those who in given circumstances must be consulted by the superior before taking action.

maintain that the law is not concerned with the validity or invalidity which would result from not complying with the formality of hearing the parties specified, but solely with the secondary purpose of contrasting the effects of advice and consent.[37] Opposed to this interpretation are those authors who hold for a strict interpretation of the law and demand the consultation as necessary for validity.[38]

The importance of the discussion concerning the interpretation of canon 105, 1°, in relation to the division of parishes cannot be overemphasized. This is true in view of the fact that historically the dividing of a parish has been considered an extreme measure, and despite a general relaxation in the strictness of the interpretation through the centuries a definite trend has manifested itself toward determining that causes definitely exist for a division. Hence, it is the opinion of the writer that the stricter view prevails in this case.

In a long discussion of the interpretation of canon 105, 1°, Ojetti (1862-1932) demonstrated very effectively that both the grammatical and the logical interpretation of the law tend to prove the stricter view the more tenable one.[39] He insisted that the text must be considered in the text and context, in answer to the opinion of Vermeersch-Creusen, namely that the law merely speaks of what is sufficient, and not of what is necessary for validity.[40] Canon 18 constituted the primary source for his argument. Using commentators on the older law to strengthen his position, Ojetti further maintained that prior to the Code it was the lot of any action when performed without the required consultation to result in invalidity.[41]

In view of the very strong extrinsic support for the stricter interpretation, as well as in consequence of the intrinsic reasons drawn from the law itself, and of the severity with which the law deals with the division of a parish when accomplished without a

---

[37] Vermeersch-Creusen, *Epitome,* I, n. 229, footnote; Ayrinhac, *Administrative Legislation,* p. 328.

[38] Ojetti, *Commentarium in Codicem Iuris Canonici* (4 vols., Romae: Universitas Gregoriana, 1927-1931), II, 180; Coronata, *Institutiones Iuris Canonice,* II, n. 983, footnote 8; De Meester, *Compendium,* Vol. III, pars I, n. 1410; Rossi, *De Paroecia,* p. 30.

[39] *Jus Pontificium* (Romae, 1921-1940), VII (1927), 13-25.

[40] Vermeersch-Creusen, *Epitome,* I, n. 229.

[41] Ojetti, *loc. cit.;* Reiffenstuel, Lib. II, tit. 10, n. 10; Schmalzgrueber, Lib. III, tit. 10, n. 10.

canonical cause, it seems that a valid division will require for validity the consultation with the parties named in canon 1428, 1.[42]

ARTICLE 2. ASSURANCE OF SUFFICIENT INCOME FOR THE NEW PARISH

Canon 1427, 3. Paroeciam dividens, Ordinarius debet vicariae perpetuae aut paroeciae noviter erectae congruam portionem assignare, servato praescripto can. 1500; quae, nisi aliunde haberi queat, desumi debet ex reditibus ad ecclesiam matricem quoquo modo pertinentibus, dummodo sufficientes reditus eidem matrici ecclesiae remaneant.

One of the chief problems to be solved by the bishop before he divides a parish is the one that is related to the financing of the new parish. The law indicates several sources to which he may look for revenue,[43] and prohibits the erection of any benefice without a certain and stable endowment which will endure permanently.[44] The new parish is to become a moral person capable of enjoying income and of bearing indebtedness, and the law seeks to safeguard the origin of the benefice lest its permanence, effectiveness, and very existence be impaired before it begins operation. Consequently, the bishop who divides a parish must investigate the funds immediately available, or of whose availability in the foreseeable future he is morally certain before he issues the decree which establishes the new parish. In that decree, he must state the source or sources of revenue.[45]

Before a definite decision can be made concerning the amount of

[42] Fanfani, *De Iure Parochorum,* p. 469; Augustine, *The Canonical and Civil Status of Catholic Parishes in the United States,* p. 168, footnote 53. Cf. Bastnagel, *The Appointment of Parochial Adjutants and Assistants,* The Catholic University of America Canon Law Studies, n. 58 (Washington, D. C.: The Catholic University of America, 1930), pp. 206-228, for a full discussion and a comparative study of the authors who take sides in the controversy.

[43] Canons 1427, § 3; 1500, 1410; 1415, § 3.

[44] Canon 1415, § 1.

[45] Canon 1418; Mothon, *Institutions Canoniques* (3 vols., Paris, 1922-1924), I, n. 211.

revenue necessary, the needs of the new parish will require some study. Not every division will entail the same building program, for example. Some new parishes must proceed immediately to building a school, a convent, a church, and a rectory, while others may need only a church and a rectory at the time the division is made. In some cases a church and a rectory may already exist, as often happens when mission churches attached to a parish are given a limited autonomy, and thus there is removed a large initial expense from consideration at the time when the division is made.[46]

Ordinarily, however, there is no ready-made church or rectory in the new parish. There is need of the purchase of land on which to build the various parish units, and the location of the property will condition the price that will have to be paid. The number of the faithful to be accommodated must be considered, and the plans for the church worked out accordingly. Arrangements must be made for the school children, either through the erection of a new school or through provisions for their transportation to the old one. Expenses of this type, plus other accidental ones, must be anticipated prior to the decision concerning the endowment of the new parish.

The law establishes a graduated scale of sources of revenue to provide the *congrua portio* for the new parish. First of all mention is made of those things which can constitute the endowment of any benefice, and then more particularly of the various means an ordinary may employ to finance new parishes. The endowment of a benefice may be composed of goods owned by a moral person, of definite payments due the benefice by some family or moral person, of voluntary but assured contributions from the faithful, or of stole fees as determined by diocesan statutes or legitimate custom.[47] If these are not available, or if when taken singly or collectively, they prove insufficient, the ordinary may make up the necessary balance or the entire endowment by using the common property and funds of the mother church, provided that a sufficient future revenue can be anticipated.[48]

The norm which will control the decision of the bishop must be

[46] Cf. Beste, *Introductio in Codicem,* p. 705.

[47] Canon 1410.

[48] Canon 1415, § 3.

the amount of endowment necessary to supply the needs of the parish and to provide a proper support for the pastor. This does not mean that the new parish must be debt-free from the moment it begins to exist, but simply that it be secure in its financial condition, entirely capable of shouldering a debt which can be retired within a reasonable length of time. Consequently the measures permitted by law for the obtaining of the initial capital, or at least of ample funds with which to begin work on the physical plant will be adopted or rejected according to the particular circumstances of the case.

As did the earlier law,[49] so the Code aims at providing for the expenses which spring from the material elements involved in divine worship, and for the livelihood of the ministers.[50] Furthermore, the endowment to be supplied must be certain and perpetual, not subject in any way to the danger of loss.[51] The Code makes no attempt to determine even approximately how much will suffice to constitute this endowment. That amount is variable with relation to the different times and places. It may be noted here that the present law allows a division even when there is no possibility of endowment in the form of capital, as long as the necessary support is morally certain to come from other sources.[52] The development of this consideration will be undertaken later in this article.

1. Endowment

> **Canon 1410.—Dotem beneficii constituunt sive bona quorum proprietas est penes ipsum ens iuridicum, sive certae et debitae praestationes alicuius familiae vel personae moralis, sive certae et voluntariae fidelium oblationes, quae ad beneficii rectorem spectent, sive iura, ut dicitur, stolae intra fines taxationis dioecesanae vel legitimae consuetudinis, . . .**

The division of a parish has as its chief effect the erection of a new benefice, and every benefice must have a distinct endowment

[49] Const. of Pope Gelasius—c. 23, c. XII, q. 2; Conc. Trident., sess. XXIV, *de ref.*, c. 13.

[50] Vermeersch-Creusen, *Epitome*, III, n. 757.

[51] Canon 1415, § 1; S.C.C., *Quebecen.*, 14 iul. 1917—*AAS*, X (1918), 196.

[52] Canon 1415, § 3.

which is joined with an ecclesiastical office, in this case the office of pastor.[53] Strictly taken, an endowment can be defined as the sum total of all the goods or obligations from which revenues are produced.[54] A descriptive definition would be this: An endowment consists of a trust fund assigned by one or more persons to the ownership of a moral person to cover the expenses of building and maintenance of the church and other buildings and of the support for the pastor, or of goods of any kind, preferably immovables, although such things as bonds are acceptable, provided that the income from the goods be certain and perpetual.[55]

The endowment system is the most satisfactory method of supplying the material necessities of the Church, since it removes most of the uncertainty from the future concerning the financial support of the parish by offering a secure income. Very early in her history the Church encouraged laymen to build and endow churches, and in return granted certain privileges regarding the appointment of the clergy who were attached to these churches.[56] The system of patronage, evolving from the desire of the Church to promote lay interest in financing parishes, endured for centuries. Experience has demonstrated that patronage can lead to serious administrative difficulties, and the present law prohibits any future institution of that kind, while at the same time it restricts already existing rights as far as possible.[57] The Church, however, still manifests approval for the establishment of endowments, as canon 1410 indicates and canon 1450 definitely demonstrates. Spiritual favors, either temporary or perpetual, may now be granted by the ordinary as a mark of gratitude for the liberality of the founder of a benefice or for the builders of churches.[58] Even more, the Church permits the

[53] Coronata, *Institutiones Iuris Canonici,* II, n. 974.

[54] Coronata, *loc. cit.*

[55] Leurenius, *Forum Beneficiale,* Vol. I, Pars I, q. 8; Wernz, *Jus Decretalium,* III, n. 182; Connolly, *The Canonical Erection of Parishes,* p. 79; De Meester, *Compendium,* Vol. III, pars I, n. 1394.

[56] Godfrey, *The Right of Patronage according to the Code of Canon Law,* The Catholic University of America Canon Law Studies, n. 21 (Washington, D. C.: The Catholic University of America, 1924), p. 64.

[57] Canon 1450.

[58] Canon 1450, §§ 1 and 2; Kremer, *Church Support in the United States,* p. 69.

ordinary to allow the founders, prior to the actual agreement with the bishop, to annex certain conditions to their grants although these conditions be contrary to the common law, with the provision, however, that they are neither unbecoming nor repugnant to the nature of a parish.[59]

If the endowment consists of a sum of money, the law obliges the ordinary, after consultation with his board of administration,[60] to invest the money in reliable and fruitful real estate or bonds.[61]

Goods which are not money or lands could be forests, vineyards, mines, quarries, and the like, which have the characteristics of stability and perpetuity demanded by the law.[62]

The second source of endowment stated in canon 1410 is that which arises from certain payments due the benefice from some family or moral person. Monasteries, other parishes, or corporations could be the moral persons in this case. For example, perhaps a mining corporation or an oil company endows a church in order to encourage men to move to rather remote localities to work for the firm. The obligation to make such payments can arise from a contract, a will, or the obligation of restitution.[63] Such payments must be certain and legally enforceable before they can be claimed as an endowment.

Under this type of plan for endowing a parish would come state support of Church institutions. The state is a moral person, and once it has made a contract for rendering payments there is constituted a permanent and stable source of revenue. The salary paid the priest by the civil government, and the agreement to supply the necessary funds to keep churches in good repair and otherwise to supply the financial needs of the parish, certainly satisfy all the requirements for the endowment of a benefice.[64] Most frequently,

---

[59] Canon 1417, § 1.

[60] Canon 1520.

[61] Canon 1415, § 2. Cf. Wernz, *Jus Decretalium,* III, n. 153; Ayrinhac, *Administrative Legislation,* p. 317.

[62] Beste, *Introductio in Codicem,* p. 697; S.C.C., *Canarien.,* 16 iul. 1927—*AAS* (1928), 389 ff.

[63] Coronata, *Institutiones Iuris Canonici,* II, n. 974.

[64] Cf. Coronata, *op. cit.,* II, n. 974; De Meester, *Compendium,* Vol. III, pars I, n. 1397; Pistocchi, *De Re Beneficiale,* pp. 20 and 21.

because of the danger of infringement on the rights of the Church that may arise from such an arrangement, the regulations for the civil support for religion are determined through a concordat.[65]

In the third place, the law allows the bishop to declare as an endowment for the new parish the certain and voluntary contributions of the faithful, which accrue to the rector for parochial purposes.[66] This type of endowment constitutes a departure from the older concept of a certain source of revenue annexed to an ecclesiastical office, since it is based on assured future contributions rather than an already existing source. But no difficulty should be encountered from this concept when it is known that the faithful because of their training and the prevailing customs recognize as a serious one their obligation to contribute to the support of the parish church. Coronata puts it well when he says that the good character of the people and their laudably formed customs are the guaranteed endowment in this case.[67] Canon 1415, § 3, considers the reliance of the bishop on the good will and generosity of the people as sufficient to allow him to proceed to the erection of a new parish.

The form which the contributions of the faithful may take are not set down in the law itself, and consequently there are many ways in which they may be sought. Historically, the scriptural system of tithes was used.[68] This procedure called for the contribution of one-tenth of all profits derived either from annual crops (praedial tithes) or personal industry (personal tithes) to the support of religion. By the sixth century Church law regulated the system.[69] Although this method of securing funds is exceptional in modern times, there can still be found some parishes which depend on the payment of tithes for their support.[70]

---

[65] Vermeersch-Creusen, *Epitome,* II, n. 743.

[66] Canon 1410.

[67] *Institutiones Iuris Canonici,* II, n. 974, c.

[68] Deuteronomy, XIV; Leviticus, XXVII.

[69] Cc. 1-35, X, *de decimis, primitiis et oblationibus,* III, 30; Doheny, *Church Property: Modes of Acquisition,* The Catholic University of America Canon Law Studies, n. 41 (Washington, D. C.: The Catholic University of America, 1927), p. 46.

[70] S.C. Consist., Resol., *Tarvisina et Patavina,* 16 iul. 1932—*AAS,* XXV (1933), 470-472. Cf. Kremer, *Church Support in the United States,* p. 37, for examples of the use of tithes in the U. S.

Most generally, however, in the United States and also in other countries which rely upon the voluntary contributions of the faithful for the support of the pastor and of the physical plant of the parish these contributions are made in the form of pew rent, offertory collections, special collections for the school, for fuel, and the like. Although the sum total of these collections will vary from year to year, they are still assured and certain, and consequently qualify as a source of endowment. Usually the total of the voluntary contributions is swelled through various types of festivals, parish socials, and other forms of socio-economic entertainments, to which the people contribute. It may be noted here that the Church allows a wide discretion in the means to be employed for the securing of additional revenue,[71] but positively forbids collecting entrance fees at the door of the church.[72] There is no penal sanction attached by the present law to the obligations of supporting the Church, but Catholics for the most part do recognize that they are morally obliged to contribute.[73] In the United States, Catholic institutions everywhere witness this recognition and manifest very tangibly that the confidence of bishops regarding future supports rests on a most solid foundation.

Stole fees as a source of endowment offered some difficulty before the Code,[74] but it is now clear that ordinaries may designate them as such and establish them as part of the parochial patrimony.[75] Canon 1410 allows for an exception to the general rule of the common law that pastors are entitled to stole fees as their own personal property,[76] and as a remuneration for special services not inherently demanded for the fulfillment of an obligation arising from his benefice or from his position as administrator of the parish property.[77] Inasmuch as the pastor has this right it seems that

---

[71] Kremer, *Church Support in the United States,* pp. 38-54.

[72] Canon 1181.

[73] Hannan, "The Obligation of Church Support"—*The Jurist* (Washington, D. C.: The Catholic University of America, 1941-), I (1941), 343-344.

[74] Wernz, *Jus Decretalium,* III, n. 183.

[75] Canon 1410; S.C.C., *Quebecen.,* 14 iul. 1917—*AAS,* X (1918), 198.

[76] Canons 463 and 1507, § 1.

[77] Connolly, *The Canonical Erection of Parishes,* p. 82.

only when other sources of endowment cannot be found or do not provide a sufficient support should ordinaries decree stole fees to be a part of the endowment of a parish.[78] Some dioceses do, as a matter of fact, state that stole fees belong to the parish treasury.[79] In such circumstances the salary of the pastor is partially at least supplied by the stole fees, since indirectly they are returned to him under another title.

Ordinaries, however, will not take away a privilege granted by the law unless necessity compels such a course of action. In the event that stole fees are included in the endowment of the parish then only the amount stipulated by the diocesan law or legitimate custom need be surrendered by the pastor. When the faithful spontaneously make more generous offerings, then the pastor is permitted to retain the excess amount.[80] Purely personal obligations arising from the acceptance of Mass stipends cannot be included in the endowment, since they are in no way connected with the benefice,[81] and belong, not to the beneficiary as such, but to the celebrant.[82]

The sources of endowment named in canon 1410 are to be considered disjunctively, and not cumulatively, that is each provision of the law is to be examined with a view to determining whether it could serve as the exclusive source of revenue for the new parish. In the event that one will not suffice, the others may be established by the bishop in whole or in part for supplying the deficiencies.[83]

This analysis of the sources of revenue which the law declares

---

[78] S.C.C., *Canarien.*, 16 iul. 1927, n. 3—*AAS*, XX (1928), 391.

[79] *Statuta Archidioecesis Sancti Francisci Lata ac Promulgata ab Excellentissimo ac Reverendissimo Joanne J. Mitty Archiepiscopo Sancti Francisci in Synodo Dioecesana Secunda* (San Francisco: The Monitor Publishing Co., 1936), nn. 69, 141, 144.

[80] Ferry, *Stole Fees*, The Catholic University of America Canon Law Studies, n. 59 (Washington, D. C.: The Catholic University of America, 1930), p. 61; Beste, *Introductio in Codicem*, p. 697.

[81] Ayrinhac, *Administrative Legislation*, p. 313.

[82] Vermeersch-Creusen, *Epitome*, II, n. 743. Cf. Wernz, *Jus Decretalium*, III, n. 183.

[83] De Meester, *Compendium*, Vol. III, pars I, n. 1394; Vermeersch-Creusen, *Epitome*, II, n. 743; Cappello, *Summa Iuris Canonici*, II, n. 534, 2.

available for the constituting of a beneficial endowment would be incomplete apart from a consideration of the particular added sources which are designated by the Code when parishes are concerned. Consequently, a further discussion is necessary concerning the wider discretion granted to ordinaries in the matter of determining ways and means for the support of a newly established parish which has resulted from the act of dividing an older parish.

2. Division of Common Property According to Canon 1500

> **Canon 1500.—Diviso territorio personae moralis ecclesiasticae its ut vel illius pars alii personae morali uniatur, vel distincta persona moralis pro parte dismembrata erigatur, etiam bona communia quae in commodum totius territorio contractum fuerat, ab auctoritate ecclesiastica, cui divisio competat, cum debita proportione ex bone et aequo dividi debent, salvis piorum fundatorum seu oblatorum voluntatibus, iuribus legitime quaesitis, ac legibus pecularibus, quibus persona moralis regatur.**

The special nature of parishes has given rise to a general broadening of the concept of endowment with which bishops must concern themselves when dividing a parish. Canon 1427, § 3, obliges ordinaries to observe the prescriptions of canon 1500 whenever they begin to consider the financing of a new parish. By reason of this canon all common property and all common debts must be divided proportionately. The common property under consideration here consists of all the funds or assets which had been destined for the benefit of the entire community, funds, for example, which had been intended for the care of the sick, the poor, the education of children, or special funds set aside for a common purpose.[84]

The property must be of such a nature that it has not become a part of the common treasury of the parish, and that it does not exist as an income which in deriving from some invested parish property is destined for the support of the church itself. Both of these sources of support constitute the proper endowment of the existing parish, and as such cannot be declared common property.

---

[84] Cf. De Meester, *Compendium,* Vol. III, pars I, n. 1410.

Hence, common property consists of any special funds or property which have as their ultimate end an extra-parochial purpose, the Peter's Pence collections for example, or functions which will benefit the parish as a whole. A monthly or a weekly special collection which looks to the gradual amassing of funds for a building project would fit the description of common property.

On the other hand, any fund destined for a particular purpose, such as the repair or the decoration of the old church, the installation of an organ or of stained glass windows, could not be disturbed.[85] By the same token a fund created by a very generous donor who earmarked the donation and its revenue for a particular local purpose would escape all possible allocation to other purposes. This includes property given by a benefactor in behalf of the poor of a certain section of the city for a recreation ground, for example, or a plot of land within the territory of the mother church when it must serve some limited exclusive purpose.[86] Exemptions of property burdened with purposes based on the particular wishes of pious lay donors from the property which can be and must be divided reflect the desire of the legislator to safeguard acquired rights and the intentions of the donors. If a moral person is concerned with the donation, a religious institute for example, special laws governing it must be observed.[87]

Often it may happen that property which is destined for the use of the entire parish has become invested in some fruitful income-producing bonds, real estate, or stocks, so that at the time of the division it would not be considered good business to convert the investment into cash. Could the new parish claim a proportionate and equitable share of the funds obtained from a later sale of the property concerned, even many years later? It seems that such property comes under the definition of common property, so that thereby the new parish is entitled to a share at the later date. Provisions for such a sharing would have to be made at the time of the division, so it seems, since the source and the assets of the endowment of a parish are to be clearly determined before the

---

[85] Beste, *Introductio in Codicem*, p. 725.

[86] See Ayrinhac, *Administrative Legislation*, pp. 387-388.

[87] Cf. Cappello, *Summa Iuris Canonici*, III, n. 546.

division actually occurs. It seems obligatory, then, for the ordinary to certify the claim of the new parish in the formal decree of its erection. In this decree he will list the source or sources of the revenue, and thus protect the endowment guaranteed by law.

Debts which have been contracted for the entire parish follow the same principles of division as those which govern the division of assets. Consequently, any obligations which were undertaken for the total number of persons in the old parish, for every parishioner in other words, must be fulfilled by those for whom they were contracted, even though some of them belong to a new parish. It would be most unjust in many cases to burden a small group in the Mother parish with debts which were contracted by a much larger group for their ultimate payment.[88] Moreover, when benefits for which liabilities have been incurred will continue to apply to all the parishioners, both of the old and of the new parish, the debt is to be divided. A school, cemetery, hospital, home for the aged, for example, to be shared by both parishes must be financed by both. This would not be true when one or the other parish would have sole possession and use of the project for which the debt was contracted, since then the debt would no longer be a common encumbrance.[89]

Canon 1500 rules that the common property and common debts of the mother church are to be divided *ex bono et aequo*. In other words, a just and equitable apportionment of funds and debts is to be made. To accomplish such a division, careful consideration must be given to the number of people involved, the needs of the new parish, and the financial status of the people involved, so that there will be established as closely as possible a proportionate balance based on the number of people in each parish. Thus, if one-third of the persons in the old parish are affected by the division, about one-third of the common funds and debts, all things being equal, should be allotted the new parish. Mathematical exactness usually will not be warranted, inasmuch as the attendant circumstances will suggest an equitable division rather than a cent

[88] Cf. Augustine, *A Commentary on Canon Law,* VI, 511.
[89] Connolly, *The Canonical Erection of Parishes,* p. 85.

for cent apportionment.[90] The demands made by particular legislation and the claims which are inherent in acquired rights can forestall the arithmetical division, as the law plainly states.[91] The ordinary must judge each case thoroughly. He will determine the relative importance and conditions of the divided territory, and allot the funds and debts accordingly.

The superior who makes the division of the territory is empowered by the law to divide the property and the indebtedness. Certainly he who by his investigation has determined that a division is necessary and warranted by the law is the one who is the most familiar with all the circumstances of the case, and therefore best fitted to decide the final apportionment of the goods and liabilities. He need not consult the so-called interested parties who must be called in when the causes for a division are under study; but when there is danger that vested rights will be injured or that equity may be sacrificed, then the persons concerned have a right to be heard.[92]

From a decree of the Sacred Congregation of the Council it appears that property and debts do not pass to a moral person by an automatic operation of law. By means of a separate act the bishop must declare what funds the new parish is to receive, and what debts it is to share with the mother parish.[93]

3. *Division Based on Anticipated Support for the New Parish*

> **Canon 1415, § 3. Non prohibetur tamen Ordinarius, ubi congrua dos constitui nequeat, pareoceas aut quasiparoecias erigere, si prudenter praevideat ea quae necessaria sunt aliunde non defutura.**

In the absence of an endowment in the strict sense for the new parish, and when all possible compliance with the provisions of canon 1500 either does not suffice or is excluded from application,

---

[90] Cf. Augustine, *A Commentary on Canon Law,* VI, 559; Ayrinhac, *Administrative Legislation,* p. 338; Beste, *Introductio in Codicem,* p. 725.

[91] Canon 1500.

[92] Pistocchi, *De Re Beneficiale,* p. 120.

[93] S.C.C., Resol., *Tarvisina et Patavina,* 16 iul. 1932—*AAS,* XXV (1933), 470-472.

and there is no other source of revenue from which an ordinary may seek the needed support, the law nevertheless allows the division of a parish, provided that moral certainty exists that the future income will be sufficient to supply the needs of the new parish. The negative wording of the canon indicates the reluctance of the legislator to make this concession. Obviously, the law has been made to allow bishops a wide discretion for determining when the salvation of souls demands a new parish. The departure from the traditional conservative tendencies of the Church concerning the necessity of a ready endowment before the creation of a benefice manifests her solicitude to satisfy as thoroughly as possible the needs of the faithful.[94]

It is to be noted that the law does not oblige the ordinary to divide a parish when funds are lacking, but merely permits it in such a case. The final decision to proceed with the division is left to his prudent judgment that the circumstances warrant confidence in a sufficient future income. Moreover, the canon does not dispense absolutely from the entire endowment, but only from a fully suitable one.[95] Consequently, it can be said that the endowment exists *in spe* rather than *in actu,* as based on the prudent judgment of the ordinary that there will be a sufficient revenue forthcoming in the future to care for the needs of the priests and the parish property.[96]

Perpetual maintenance of the parish and its ministers must be morally certain, and in this respect § 3 of Canon 1415 does not differ from § 1 of the same canon, in which it is forbidden to erect any benefice without a perpetual suitable endowment. The chief difference between the two paragraphs is that in the first the endowment or source of income is permanently and specifically determined at the time of division, while in the other no such determination is made.[97]

---

[94] Beste, *Introductio in Codicem,* p. 699.

[95] Coronata, *Institutiones Iuris Canonici,* II, n. 978.

[96] Cappello, *Summa Iuris Canonici,* II, n. 538.

[97] Cf. Coronata, *Institutiones Iuris Canonici,* II, n. 978; Cappello, *Summa Iuris Canonici,* II, n. 538; Connolly, *The Canonical Erection of Parishes,* pp. 89-90.

The bishop, however, must have some guarantee of an adequate future income for the new parish, a guarantee which he could strengthen by indicating various sources of revenue. For example, the people who will benefit by the new parish could be exhorted to contribute generously to secure some initial funds,[98] or he could draw from a diocesan mission fund or some similar foundation when the faithful are very poor and unable to contribute. If it is known that the people concerned are willing to make substantial donations in the future, the ordinary may proceed as in possession of the required certitude. Certainly, too, if the number of parishioners is large enough to assure ample stole fees, the latter could be considered reasonably to constitute insurance that the pastor will not lack proper support.[99]

Another alternative remaining to the ordinary is to unite to the pastorate some other benefice which does not involve the care of souls or the obligation of residence.[100] The law allows bishops to do this.[101] For example, a mass foundation erected by the bishop could be united to the parish. A chaplaincy in a hospital or in some subsidiary church could likewise be granted.[102] Since the bishop has the obligation to obtain certainty that the future income will be made and perpetual, the final decision must rest with him concerning the most effective means to provide for the situation.

When there is no assurance that even the minimum requirements can be prudently foreseen, the bishop may do no more than designate "mission" churches or chaplaincies within the boundaries of the parish upon which they shall remain dependent until such time as a sufficient income is assured for their independent existence.[103]

The Pontifical Commission for the Interpretation of the Code

---

[98] Cf. canon 1186, 2°.

[99] Beste, *Introductio in Codicem*, p. 699; Ayrinhac, *Administrative Legislation*, p. 317.

[100] Cf. Conc. Trident., sess. XXIV, *de ref.*, c. 13.

[101] Canons 1419, § 3; 1420, § 3; and 1423, § 1.

[102] Cf. Beste, *Introductio in Codicem*, p. 702.

[103] S.C. Consist., *declar.* 1 aug. 1919—*AAS*, XI (1918), 346; Coronata, *Institutiones Iuris Canonici*, II, n. 978.

has removed all doubts concerning the canonical status of parishes in the United States. It declared that all parishes having "(1) a resident pastor; (2) an endowment (resources or revenue according to the provisions of canons 1410 or 1415, § 3); and (3) boundaries," are not only parishes in the strict sense, but are also ecclesiastical benefices.[104] Consequently the practice, common in the United States, of dividing parishes and depending entirely on canon 1415, § 3, for the legal provisions regarding endowment can be sanctioned. But at the same time it seems a closer correspondence to the demands of equity, if not also of justice, to use wherever possible, the ordinary sources of revenue, especially since the law indicates strongly its preference for a specific endowment.[105] The reluctant wording of canon 1415, § 3, implies that the application of its ruling should constitute a last resort. Hence, when the old parish has sufficient revenue to allow for a substantial apportionment of funds to the new parish according to canon 1500, or when the sources of revenue indicated in canon 1410 can supply its needs, the tenor of the law seems primarily to call for the utilization of these resources in behalf of the new parish.

Very often the division of parishes in this country involves great financial difficulties. Usually the existing parishes are not clear of debt, and the goods consist of the voluntary offerings of the faithful and little else.[106] The heavy debts which a new parish must necessarily incur will place a very heavy burden on the parishioners, and it scarcely seems just to ask the new parish to assume any part of the debt of the mother church as well. In localities where the good of souls demands a rather rapid multiplication of parishes, exclusive dependence on the ruling of canon 1415, § 3, can become necessary. Ordinaries have learned that the faithful are worthy of great confidence in the matter of supplying sufficient funds to support parishes and their ministers. In ordinary circumstances, then, it can be safely presumed that moral certitude will be present, so that the

---

104 Bouscaren, *The Canon Law Digest,* I, 151.

105 Canons 1409; 1410; 1427, § 3; and 1500.

106 Woywod, *A Practical Commentary,* II, 145.

bishops can permissibly divide parishes on this basis rather than by imposing double burdens on the members of the new parish.[107]

4. Relationship to the Mother Church

Canon 1427, § 4. Si vicaria perpetua aut nova paroecia dotetur ex reditibus ecclesiae a qua dividitur, debet matrici honorem deferre modo et finibus ab Ordinario praestituendis; qui tamen vetatur baptismalem fontem matrici ipsi reservare.

The law clearly indicates that a parish divided from another should pay honor in some way to the mother church when the latter endows it. Only when the ordinary has determined that the original parish is to provide the initial capital, or a portion of it, is such honor demanded.[108] So long as the revenues which belong in any way to the mother church can serve as a source of support for the new parish without danger of serious harm to the financial status of the former, the law authorizes the bishop, wherever necessary, to draw from them.[109] No type of property belonging to the mother church is exempt from assessment.

The relationship to which canon 1427, § 4, refers is one of origin, arising when one or more parishes are formed from the people and the territory of the original parish.[110] Furthermore, a church can be called "mother" only when it has provided at least part of the endowment of the filial church.[111] A combination, then, of origin and endowment in whole or in part of the new parish constitutes an *ecclesia matrix*. No permission is granted by the law for the endowing of a parish which is not filial by origin. The same prohibition obtained in the earlier law.[112]

---

[107] Cf. Coronata, *Institutiones Iuris Canonici,* II, n. 974 (c).

[108] Pistocchi, *De Re Beneficiali,* p. 122; Augustine, *The Canonical and Civil Status of Parishes,* p. 175.

[109] Canon 1427, § 3; S.C.C., *Bergomen,* 22 aug. 1908—*Thesaurus,* CLXVIII (1909), 651.

[110] S.C.C., *Caietana,* 10 aug. 1917—*AAS,* X (1918), 460.

[111] S.C.C., *Aversana, Matricitatis,* 13 iun. 1931—*AAS,* XXV (1933), 208-211; Pistocchi, *De Re Beneficiali,* p. 14, footnote.

[112] Fagnanus, Lib. III, tit. 48, c. 3, n. 32.

The precise form which the honor will take must be determined by the ordinary, and ought to be stated in the decree which establishes the new parish.[113] There is considerable departure from the old law in the present canon law as reflected in canon 1427, § 4. Decretal law conceded the right of patronage over the new parish to the rector of the mother church whenever the latter supplied the endowment of the newly erected parish.[114] There was formerly granted the permission to reserve certain signs of recognition to the mother church, signs which indicated the retention of traces of her former jurisdiction in the territory of the new parish. In view of the derived authority of the new parish and the endowment which had come from the mother church, acknowledgment was to be tendered in some way, usually through the granting of the right to conduct all funerals, to receive the tithes, or an annual tribute of some kind.[115] Other signs which were popular were the reservation of the baptismal font to the mother church, the right of the pastor of the mother church to perform certain solemn functions on specified feast days of the year, and his right to select the first pastor of the new parish.[116]

The present law, while not designating the form that the marks of honor should take, forbids the bishop to reserve the right of the baptismal font to the mother church, and at the same time commands that every parochial church have its own font, "any statute, privilege, or custom to the contrary notwithstanding."[117] Since the present law forbids all future concessions of the right of patronage,[118] the rector of the mother church could not be granted any patronal rights based on the endowment of the filial church. The right of presentation of the pastor of the new church, once accorded to the pastor of the old church, seems to have been abrogated with the publication of the Code.[119]

---

[113] Connolly, *The Canonical Erection of Parishes*, p. 88.

[114] C. 3, X, *de ecclesiis aedificandis vel reparandis*, III, 48; cf. Bouix, *De Parocho*, p. 277.

[115] Schmalzgrueber, Lib. III, tit. 49, n. 19; Rossi, *De Paroecia*, p. 32; S.C.C., *Aversana Matricitatis*, 13 iun. 1931—*AAS*, XXV (1933), 208 ff.

[116] Rossi, *loc. cit.;* Leurenius, *Forum Beneficiale*, Vol. I, pars I, a. 157, n. 7.

[117] Canon 774, § 1.

[118] Canon 1450, § 1.

[119] Canon 6, 6°; c. 3, X, *de praebendis et dignitatibus*, III, 5.

In the United States, the practice of manifesting the relationship between mother and filial church has never been followed, possibly because seldom in the past has a new church received an endowment in whole or in part from the older one. In some dioceses it is customary for the old parish to grant a lump sum of money as an outright gift to the newly established parish. It can be questioned that this gift may be regarded as constituting an endowment in the sense of canon 1410, especially when it is a relatively small amount. Consequently, the necessary elements of both a furnished endowment and also a derived origin are lacking, and hence no obligation regarding the manifestation of honor will rest upon the new parish. If, on the other hand, the bishop would designate a certain sum as an endowment, the law would then seem to hold.

It should here be noted that the Sacred Congregation of the Council frowns on the custom of foregoing the manifestation of these traditional signs of honor when both origin and endowment derive from the mother church.[120]

With the present law silent as to the precise nature of the honor to be shown, it seems that any form permitted by the former law, and not either reprobated or forbidden by the Code, would still be permissible. Consequently, bishops can order any of the traditional signs of recognition in a given case of the division of a parish when both origin and endowment derive from the mother church. Connolly suggests that a tablet which commemorates the relationship between the mother and the filial churches and is conspicuously located in the filial church would be a simple but effective means of manifesting the called for recognition.[121] The ordinary is given wide liberty to select the most appropriate means, and hence could follow the customary practice of the locality, or utilize one or the other of the older forms.

ARTICLE 3. FORMAL DECREE OF ERECTION OF THE NEW PARISH

A moral personality in the Church cannot begin to exist save by prescription of the law itself or else by a special concession of a

[120] S.C.C., *Caetana,* 10 aug. 1917—*AAS,* X (1918), 453 ff. Cf. *Nouvelle Revue Theologique* (Tournai, 1869-), XXXII (1900), 552.

[121] *The Canonical Erection of Parishes,* p. 89.

competent ecclesiastical superior given by means of a formal decree.[122] Parishes are canonical moral units within the Church, deriving their existence from her authority, and therefore must be designated as such by ordinaries who rule over dioceses.[123] The Code itself is silent about the act by which parishes are founded, simply ordering that dioceses are to be divided.[124] When all the elements prescribed, namely a distinct territory, a community of the faithful, a proper pastor, and a church are present, the law recognizes these combined elements as constituting a parish.

Although nowhere does the Code explicitly demand a formal decree for the erection of a parish newly divided from another, canon 1418 clearly demands that benefices be established by means of a document in which the location of the benefice is to be stated, its endowment determined, and its rights and obligations described. Furthermore, canon 1428, § 1, prescribes that all modification of parishes be made by means of an authentic written document. Since parishes are benefices, canon 1418 must be applied, and the later canon, namely canon 1428, § 1, more specifically applies to the division of parishes and requires written proof that the division has been effected.[125]

A decree of the Sacred Consistorial Congregation made it necessary that a decree of the ordinary be issued when new parishes were established in what were formerly mission dioceses.[126] A similar regulation was issued by the Sacred Congregation for the Propagation of the Faith for mission territories.[127]

Undoubtedly, then, the lawful founding of a parish can be effected only by means of a formal decree of the local ordinary. This decree must determine accurately the location of the parish

---

[122] Canon 100, § 1.

[123] Cf. Brown, *The Canonical Juristic Personality with Special Reference to its Status in the United States of America,* The Catholic University of America Canon Law Studies, n. 38 (Washington, D. C.: The Catholic University of America, 1927), pp. 91-92.

[124] Canon 216, § 1.

[125] Ayrinhac, *Administrative Legislation,* p. 324.

[126] S.C. Consist., declar., 1 aug. 1919, n. 2—*AAS,* XI (1919), 346. Cf. also S.C. de Prop. Fide, decr. 9 dec. 1920, n. 2—*AAS,* XIII (1921), 18.

[127] S.C. Prop. Fide. instr. 25 iul. 1920, nn. 4, 5—*AAS,* XII (1920), 332.

by clearly stating its boundaries, thereby eliminating completely potential difficulties in that regard. The site of the parish church must be accurately set down. The endowment, if any, and its source or sources should be delineated. And finally, the status of the pastor, whether removable or irremovable, is to be determined.[128] Included in the decree, when the mother church has contributed at least partially to the endowment of the new parish, should be a statement of the form which the token of honor prescribed by law is to take.[129]

Although the formal decree by which the new parish receives its independent existence is not the same thing as the authentic document, by means of which the parish is constituted,[130] usually the decree becomes public through the document itself, and consequently in practice they are equivalent. The document, strictly considered, bears proof of the act of the bishop, in that it certifies the division of the new parish from the mother church and at the same time includes mention of the essential elements mentioned above. In this way all the facts pertinent to the new parish are recorded, uncertainties are removed, and a permanent official document is preserved for future reference in the event that difficulties should arise.

Diocesan records are public documents in the ecclesiastical courts,[131] but in the United States official recognition by the State is denied inasmuch as bishops and other Church officials are not accorded the necessary acceptance by the civil government in consequence of the absence of official relations between the Church and the various states.[132] If a diocese or a parish has availed itself of the right to form a private corporation, the bishop or the pastor is accepted as the head of that corporation with rights recognized and protected according to the secular law.[133] Consequently, good business as well as prudent administration seems to demand not only a formal document which attests the existence of the new ecclesias-

---

[128] Canon 1418; S.C. Consist., declar., 1 aug. 1919—*AAS,* XI (1919), 346.

[129] Canon 1427, § 4; Connolly, *The Canonical Erection of Parishes,* p. 88.

[130] S.C.C., *Principis Alberten. et Saskatoonen., Missae pro populo,* 5 mart. 1932—*AAS,* XXV (1933), 436-438.

[131] Canon 1813.

[132] Woywod, *A Practical Commentary,* II, 285.

[133] Woywod, *A Practical Commentary,* II, p. 285.

tical moral person, with rights and duties definitely defined, but also a document which fully complies with the demands of the civil law.[134] Also the formal ecclesiastical document should be notarized by the chancellor of some other ecclesiastical notary, and in this country a notary public should also certify the writ to add civil sanction to its effects.[135]

At no time in history has law demanded the formal decree as a condition for the validity of the foundation of a parish. The Sacred Congregation of the Council held in the last century that the canonical constitution of a parish did not depend entirely on a formal decree, but that it also resulted from the presence of the other elements which if they exist together, constitute a parish, namely, a territory with well-defined boundaries, a community of the faithful, a pastor, and the authority of the bishop stating or approving the erection of the new parish.[136]

The old discipline is still maintained in view of the fact that the present law makes no mention of invalidity as attaching to the failure to issue such a decree, and canon 11 rules out the branding of an act as null and void unless the law itself declares it such expressly or equivalently. Furthermore, a reply of Cardinal Gasparri to the Apostolic Delegate to the United States regarding the status of parishes in this country declared that a special decree of the ordinary is not necessary for the establishment of a new parish, but that it suffices for the ordinary to supply all the necessary elements of a parish.[137] Another decree of the Sacred Congregation of the Council, since the Code was promulgated, pointed out that by attributing to a parish the titles, rights, and obligations that can belong only to a parish the bishop had given an implicit decree erecting the new parish.[138]

---

[134] Vermeersch-Creusen, *Epitome,* II, n. 750; Augustine, *A Commentary on Canon Law,* VI, 500.

[135] Cappello, *Summa Iuris Canonici,* II, n. 373; Beste, *Introductio in Codicem,* p. 700.

[136] S.C.C., litt. 18 mart. 1881—*Coll. S.C.P.F.,* n. 1548.

[137] Bouscaren, *The Canon Law Digest,* I, 149-151.

[138] S.C.C., *Principis Alberten. et Saskatoonen.,* 5 mart. 1932—*AAS,* XXV (1933), 436-438; cf. Maroto for a commentary on this response in *Apollinaris* (Romae, 1928-), VI (1933), 423-431.

Modern authors are almost unanimous in teaching that a document is necessary, but none urges the necessity as affecting the validity of the act of the bishop.[139]

The present law declares that when a prefecture or vicariate apostolic becomes a diocese, its quasi-parishes automatically become parishes, and there is no need of a decree for effecting the change.[140]

A problem arises concerning the content of the decree through which the new parish is established. Once the preliminary legal requirements have been carefully completed, the document should be issued. It is to list the various elements necessary for the proper constitution of the parish. Ordinarily no difficulty should be experienced concerning the boundaries. These should be fixed clearly, permanently, and immutably.[141] No transitory objects should be designated as boundaries, since they have no permanent character.[142] Hence, only natural landmarks, such as rivers, hills, lakes, and artificial permanent structures such as roads, political boundaries, railroad right-of-ways, and the like, serve in the capacity of safe boundaries.

Likewise the source or sources of the endowment, if the new parish is to be granted one according to law, should not cause any concern as long as it is clearly manifest in the decree. The location of the parish church and of the rectory can be simply stated too.

The status of the pastor, whether he be removable or irremovable, is a matter that could give rise to difficulties if a statement regarding it has been ignored in the document that witnesses the decree of the ordinary. Where would the presumption lie were mention of that status to be ignored? The law states that the pastors of new parishes are to be irremovable, unless the bishop, after consulting the cathedral chapter or the diocesan consultors, prudently judges

---

[139] Coronata, *Institutiones Iuris Canonici,* II, n. 978, 4; Vermeersch-Creusen, *Epitome,* II, n. 750; Rossi, *De Paroecia,* p. 33. An exception to the general teaching is found in Pistocchi, *De Re Beneficiali,* p. 130, who maintains that the decree and the document are necessary for validity. Cf. Reiffenstuel, Lib. III, tit. 5, nn. 102-104 for an older opinion similar to that of the majority of modern authors.

[140] Canon 216, § 3; Bouscaren, *The Canon Law Digest,* I, 150.

[141] S.R., *Bononien.,* 21 iul. 1911, N. 6—*Decisiones,* III (1911), 357.

[142] S.R., *Annecien.,* 5 febr. 1918—*AAS,* XI (1919), 146-151.

that under the peculiar circumstances of place and person a movable rectorship is more advisable, and arranges the matter accordingly.[143] Consequently, the presumption must be, in the absence of any declaration by the ordinary in the formal decree, that the parish is one of irremovable tenure. It seems rather important, then, that this element of the decree be considered carefully, lest the first incumbent assert his right when the ordinary in considering the parish a revocable one wishes to transfer or remove him. The Code very clearly indicates its desire to have future parishes irrevocable, but it allows some discretion to the ordinary and his council in the matter of determining the advisability of establishing a parish as such in a given case.[144]

Quasi-parishes are all revocable,[145] and hence the presumption stands in favor of the revocability of the new quasi-parish when nothing is stated in the decree concerning its status.

The law for the missions orders that two copies of the decree establishing the quasi-parish are to be made, one to be kept in the archives of the ordinary, the other in the files of the parish or quasi-parish.[146]

While there is nothing in the law to indicate that fully organized dioceses are to preserve records of the division of the old and the establishment of the new parish, certainly it is most necessary both from the point of view of good business and from that of fulfilling the requirement for the establishment of a new benefice. The law is clear in regard to the latter when it says "the erection of benefices is to be effected by means of a legal document, which shall define the endowment of the benefice and the rights and the obligations of the beneficiary."[147] Consequently the preservation of a record in the diocesan and parish archives seems equally demanded. In its contents the record is to incorporate more than just the points enumerated in canon 1418. It must advert to all the essential matters outlined above.

---

[143] Canon 454, § 3.

[144] Beste, *Introductio in Codicem,* p. 286.

[145] Canon 454, § 4.

[146] S.C. Prop. Fide, 25 iul. and 9 dec. 1920—*AAS,* XII (1920), 331, and XIII (1921), 17.

[147] Canon 1418.

ARTICLE 4. RECOURSE AGAINST THE DECREE OF DIVISION

Canon 1428, § 3. Adversus decretum Ordinarii unientis, transferentis, dividentis aut dismembrantis beneficia, datur in devolutivo tantum recursus ad Sanctam Sedem.

Although the Code allows ordinaries to divide parishes in the face of opposition from the pastor and without the consent of the people,[148] it protects the interests of the parochial Church and those of the people affected against the decree of a bishop which can at most be regarded as only doubtfully just. The Code states the conditions under which a parish may be divided, and leaves to the prudent judgment of the ordinary the decision regarding the existence of the canonical causes, the prospect of sufficient support, the location of the new church, and the boundaries of the new parish. No license is granted, however, to deviate from the prescriptions of law, and consequently the possibility of the lack of prudence in a particular instance is contemplated by the law when the opportunity is given to present alleged infractions of regulations for review to the Holy See.

Formerly, the action of a bishop in dividing a parish which was united *pleno iure* to a religious institute could be impugned only at the Holy See.[149] This was true because in such a division the bishop had acted as a delegate of the Holy See. In all other cases option was granted to have recourse either to Rome or to the metropolitan.[150] At first reading the Decretals appear to have forbidden all recourse against an effected division of a parish.[151] Commentators, however, were unanimous in their interpretation that the prohibition simply forbade that kind of recourse which would have suspended the action decreed by the bishop.[152]

The present law concedes ordinary power to bishops to divide

---

[148] Canon 1427, § 1.

[149] Conc. Trident., sess. XXI, *de ref.*, c. 4.

[150] Bouix, *De Parocho*, p. 282.

[151] ". . . sublato appellationis obstaculo, . . . appellationis cessante diffugio." —c. 3, X, *de ecclesiis aedificandis vel reparandis*, III, 48.

[152] Fagnanus, Lib. III, tit. 48, c. 3, nn. 45-47; Barbosa, *De officio et potestate Episcopi*, alleg. 20, n. 1; Bouix, *De Parocho*, p. 280.

all parishes, including those under the care of religious,[153] and recourse must be taken directly to the Holy See. Deviating from the old law, the Code removes competence from the metropolitan. "Against the decrees of the ordinary there is not granted any appeal or recourse to the Sacred Rota; but the Sacred Congregations exclusively handle recourses of this kind."[154] In all matters of recourse against decrees concerning the division of benefices the Sacred Congregation of the Council is competent.[155] Mission territories must look to the Sacred Congregation of the Propagation of the Faith for recourse against the division of quasi-parishes.[156]

Since the division of a parish connotes purely an administrative and not a judicial action, there is no question of an appeal in the strict canonical sense. An appeal is concerned with the attack of a sentence arrived at through judicial proceedings. Normally recourse from an administrative decree must be made to the superior designated by law, with provisions made for exceptional cases. Hypothetically, when positive reasons indicate that the Sacred Congregation of the Council has not given a just decision, the way is left open for a direct recourse to the Holy Father, who will leave the decision to the Apostolic Signatura as to whether there has been any injustice which would warrant a trial before the Rota.[157]

Concerning the competence of the Sacred Congregations to judge the decrees of ordinaries pertaining to the administration of their dioceses, the Code Commission has determined two important points. The Commission was asked whether a judicial action could be instituted, according to canons 1552-1601, against the decrees, acts and dispositions of ordinaries, appointment to benefices, offices, etc., or the refusal to make such appointments. If no such action was permitted by these canons, the question was "whether a judicial action can be instituted at least for damages resulting from such decrees, acts, and dispositions, so that the ordinary can, according to canon 1557, § 2, and canon 1559, § 2, be summoned before the

---

153 Canon 1427, § 1.

154 Canon 1601.

155 Canon 250, § 2.

156 Canon 252, § 3.

157 Canon 1603, § 2.

tribunal of the Sacred Roman Rota."[158] Both questions received negative replies. Hence competence regarding the action of a bishop and damages alleged to have resulted from that action belong exclusively to the Sacred Congregation indicated by the law. The Sacred Congregation of the Council, then, will have exclusive competence in cases of recourse against the division of a parish and any damage claims which may be submitted as having their roots in the division.[159]

A decision of the Rota, in which it disavowed its competence in a case wherein a canon wished to sue a bishop for damages before the Rota after the Sacred Congregation of the Council had denied his claim against an unjust administrative action by the bishop, confirms this interpretation. The Rota stated that "when a question has once been presented to one of the Sacred Congregations to be settled according to disciplinary procedure, and when a party has consented, or at least made no objection, to the procedure, he may not thereafter institute strictly judicial proceedings upon the same question."[160] Consequently, once a recourse is directed to the Sacred

30 apr. 1923—*AAS,* XV (1923), 296; Canon 243, § 1.

Congregation of the Council on the grounds that the division has been effected without regard for one or the other of the requirements of law, the way is closed to any later Rota action for the simple reason that only an appeal, but not a recourse, is admissible before the Rota.

The reason or occasion for taking recourse is not restricted in any way by the law, and hence the person who feels himself or the parish to have a just grievance can attack the decree on any grounds. The lack of some canonical cause, the absence of a secure endowment, the lack of assurance that a sufficient support remains for the mother church, the hardship imposed on the faithful, the injury to rights and privileges of interested persons without a sufficient cause, the impracticability of the division, and the like, would be reasons of sufficient merit for seeking a nullifying declaration from the Sacred Congregation of the Council.

---

[158] Bouscaren, *The Canon Law Digest,* I, p. 739; *AAS,* XVI (1924), 251.

[159] Beste, *Introductio in Codicem,* p. 774.

[160] Bouscaren, *The Canon Law Digest,* I, 747; S.R.R., *Sententia Incidentalis,*

The effect of the recourse is *in devolutivo,* that is, the decree of the ordinary remains in force even while the recourse is pending. But it becomes a matter of prudence, once the ordinary has been informed that recourse has been made against his decree, that he should halt building plans until the question has been settled.[161]

Recourse should be made simply by means of forwarding the petition to the Sacred Congregation in the form of a letter, although apparently it can also be made through an agency or by proxy.[162] If the person who institutes the recourse is unfamiliar with the curial language, he is permitted to write in English, German, or Portuguese, since Pius X ordered each Sacred Congregation to have auditors conversant with at least one of these tongues.[163] Clerics, especially ecclesiastical dignitaries, should always use Latin, the official language of the Church, in their letters to the Holy See.[164] The burden of proof rests with the person or persons who interpose the recourse with the Holy See, and consequently the petition should express briefly and accurately the reasons why it is believed that the act of the ordinary was unjustified in view of carefully outlined circumstances. Included with the petition should be the decree of the bishop dividing the parish.[165] Augustine suggested that it would be helpful to refer to former decisions in cases of a similar nature.[166] Topographic maps and photographs would be of considerable assistance to the Congregation when there is question of the presence of a canonical cause, or when it is alleged that there is no prospect of population growth because of the nature of the land, or when the area appears to be tending towards industrialization, and in other like instances.

In his defense the ordinary should send all reports rendered by his advisors prior to the division, with his reasons for acting as he did, and his convictions in regard to the point or points which

---

[161] McClunn, *Administrative Recourse,* The Catholic University of America Canon Law Studies, n. 240 (Washington, D. C.: The Catholic University of America Press, 1946), pp. 117-118.

[162] McClunn, *op. cit.,* p. 37.

[163] *Normae Peculiares,* Cap. VI, 5—*AAS,* I (1909), 73.

[164] Cappello, *De Curia Romana* (2 vols., Romae, 1911), I, 44.

[165] McClunn, *Administrative Recourse,* p. 42.

[166] *The Canonical and Civil Status of Catholic Parishes,* p. 180.

have been attacked. All documentary evidence or data pertaining to the case will be required in Rome.[167]

Is it necessary that the ordinary be notified by the petitioner that the decree has been attacked? The law does not demand such a notification for either the validity or the licitness of the recourse, but it appears to be advisable nonetheless if a speedy disposition of the recourse is to be accomplished. The Sacred Congregation of the Council is not likely to revoke the decree of an ordinary without hearing his views on the matter, and certainly will not act without possessing all the necessary information.[168] As soon as the notification of the recourse has been received by the ordinary, whether it be from the petitioner or from the Congregation, the required data must be sent on.

The time within which a recourse against an administrative decree of the ordinary may be instituted is not designated in the law. Pre-Code law did, as a matter of fact, state a ten-day period as the usual time allowed for the use of recourse.[169] These ten days, as provided for in Roman Law and restated by Gratian in his Decretum, were computed as a *tempus utile,* that is, as long as one was without the opportunity to make an appeal, there was no lapse of time in one's disfavor.[170] This is no longer true, and there is no time limit prescribed for the instituting of a recourse which does not involve any suspensive effect.[171]

A decree of the Sacred Congregation of the Council before the Code indicated that a recourse against an alleged injury was permitted after a lapse of almost two years.[172] The peculiar nature of the act whereby a parish is divided would however seem to demand that the recourse be instituted at an early date, namely,

---

[167] Examples of well defended cases are: S.R.R., *Sedunen.,* 2 apr. 1912—*Decisiones,* IV (1912), 149; *AAS,* IC (1912), 457 in the pre-Code law; S.C.C., *Canarien.,* 16 iul. 1927—*AAS,* XX (1928), 391 ff., in the present law.

[168] McClunn, *Administrative Recourse,* p. 38.

[169] Panormitanus, tit. *de appellationibus* (II, 8); Pirhing, Lib. III, tit. 28, n. 3.

[170] D. (49, 4), 1, Biduum; c. 29, C. II, q. 6.

[171] McClunn, *Administrative Recourse,* p. 59.

[172] S.C.C., *Concordien.,* 2 febr. 1897—*Fontes,* n. 4300.

because of the equity involved. It would be very dangerous, and very expensive, for example, to delay the recourse until work had already been begun on one or more buildings for the new parish. If the parish which is being erected has been ordered to proceed to the immediate construction of a church, it would seem to be more equitable and just, not to say demonstrative of a sincere desire to right the alleged wrong, to warn the ordinary at once of the intention to institute a recourse with the Holy See.

Who may avail themselves of the opportunity to approach the Holy See for defense against the purported unjust or inequitable division? Any member of the clergy or of the laity is free to approach the Roman Pontiff with a request for justice.[173] Hence, the pastor or any other priest attached to the mother church, as well as any of the faithful—those with or without special rights or privileges—could lodge a petition for the nullification of the decree. If damages are also sought as resulting from the action of the ordinary, the person or persons thinking themselves injured can submit a claim along with the recourse of any other petitioner who is attacking the validity of the division.[174]

The Code makes it very clear that subordinate authorities should not continue to act when the matter has been given over to a higher authority for a final judgment.[175] This prescription is based on the reverence which a subordinate authority should manifest towards its superior, and is certainly applicable to cases of recourse.[176]

Although canon 204, § 2, does not invalidate an act which is undertaken contrary to its rule, yet this rule does make such a

---

[173] Conc. Vat., sess. IV, *De Constitutione Ecclesiae*, cap. 3—Mansi, LII, 1332; Denzinger-Bannwart-Umberg, *Enchiridion Symbolorum, Definitionum, et Declarationum de Rebus Fidei et Morum* (21.-23. ed., Friburgi Brisgoviae, Herder and Co., 1937), n. 1830.

[174] Cf. McClunn, *Administrative Recourse*, p. 43.

[175] Canon 204, § 2—Attamen rei ad Superiorem delata ne se immisceat inferior, nisi ex gravi urgenti causa; et hoc in casu statim Superiorem de re moneat.

[176] Cf. Ayrinhac, *General Legislation in the New Code of Canon Law* (New York: Longmans, Green & Co., 1933), p. 362; Beste, *Introductio in Codicem*, p. 219.

contrary act illicit. Consequently the ordinary should not begin execution of his decree of division and start building until the decision of the Holy See has been notified. If the causes for erecting the new church are sufficiently urgent and grave, the ordinary may proceed, but he is obliged to notify the Sacred Congregation of the Council of his action, and should give the reasons for doing so.

CHAPTER VII

Division of Particular Types of Parishes

ARTICLE 1. DIVISION OF RELIGIOUS PARISHES

The various types of parishes which can be designated "religious" have been discussed in a previous chapter of this work.[1] In the following analysis of the law regulating the division of religious parishes no distinction will be made between parishes united either *plenissimo iure* or simply *pleno iure* with a religious institute, since the law itself makes no such distinction.

Essentially, there is no difference between a parish under the care of religious and one governed by secular priests. Only in the manner in which they come to exist,[2] and in the control which the ordinary may exercise over them,[3] can distinguishing characteristics be discerned. Consequently, when the law permits ordinaries to divide any and all parishes—*paroecias quaslibet*[4]—if the canonical requisites are present, it implies that the essential properties of parishes are of primary importance, and that when the salvation of souls justifies or demands the division of a parish the canonical status of the priests in charge, regular or secular, is of no moment.[5]

Exception to the above-mentioned rule that all parishes are subject to division by the ordinary is made in canon 216, § 4, where national, lingual, and familial parishes are described as completely under the control of the Holy See as regards their constitution and modification. The following article of this work will discuss the question of the division of such parishes.

A general principle reserving the union, transfer, division, and dismemberment of a religious benefice to the Holy See is indeed

---

[1] Cf. *supra*, chapter II, pp. 9-11.

[2] Cf. canons 215, § 1; 452, § 1; 1425, § 1; 1423, § 2.

[3] Canons 452; 456; 1425, § 2; 471, § 1.

[4] Canon 1427, § 1.

[5] Cf. Vermeersch-Creusen, *Epitome*, II, n. 754.

enunciated in the law.[6] The nature of parishes, however, calls for a more particular regulation, especially in view of the fact that a parish is more than an office and a benefice. It is a certain part of a diocese with a definitely described boundary, embracing a certain group of the faithful. Since the good of souls often demands changes in the material establishments constituted for the supplying of their needs in view of the flexible human element, temporal considerations must cede to those of a spiritual nature.

To the ordinary whose chief task it is to foster all things which prove conducive to the spiritual betterment of his flock, the law grants wide discretionary power in the matter of modifying parishes to fit particular situations. Greater power is given him in that regard than is granted when other religious benefices are concerned.[7] It can be said, then, that canon 1427, § 1, prevails as an exception to the general norm of canon 1422. The old axiom is verified in this instance—"genus per speciem derogatur."[8] Augustine remarked that probably it was the mind of the legislator to allow the exception because ordinaries have an ***intentio in iure fundata*** concerning all parishes under their jurisdiction.[9] Obviously this was the principle which guided Pope Leo XIII (1878-1903) in his decision concerning parishes in England,[10] a decision later applied to the United States,[11] in which ordinaries were granted the power to divide religious parishes and to assign the new parish to diocesan priests.

Most of the modern canonists insist on the interpretation described above for solving the apparent conflict between canons

---

[6] Canon 1422. ". . . unio aeque aut minus principalis beneficii religiosi cum saeculari et contra, itemque beneficii religiosi translatio, divisio et dismembratio quaelibet uni Sedi Apostolicae reservantur."

[7] Vermeersch-Creusen, *Epitome,* II, n. 757.

[8] Fanfani, *De Iure Parochorum,* p. 20; Augustine, *A Commentary on Canon Law,* VI, 508.

[9] *Loc. cit.*

[10] Const. *"Romanos Pontifices,"* 8 maii 1881, nn. 15 and 16—*Fontes,* n. 582. In this Constitution Pope Leo solved difficulties peculiar to the British Isles, but declared it to be merely a restatement of the common law.

[11] *Acta et Decreta Concilii Plenarii Baltimorensis Tertii* (Baltimore, 1886), p. cv.

1422 and 1427, § 1. However, Rossi[12] and Wernz-Vidal[13] maintain the opposite view, but give no reasons for their opinion. Certainly, in view of the older law which gave delegated power to ordinaries to divide parishes under the care of religious it seems that the majority opinion has the greater weight.[14] The law today makes no qualification whatsoever, nor does it restrict the power of the ordinary to divide any parish, and consequently it can be stated that the sole point of difference between the former and the present law rests in this that formerly bishops acted with delegated power, but under the present discipline proceed with ordinary power when the division of religious parishes is concerned.

The present law states that the new parishes which result from the division of religious parishes are themselves not religious parishes. There is thus implied the bishop's full capacity for the dividing of a parish which is ruled by religious.[15] The former law made similar provisions when it demanded that all new parishes be given over to the care of diocesan priests,[16] and ordered at the same time that a parish established by division from a parish with a patron should be of free conferral after the division. The present law calls for the discontinuance of the right of patronage entirely for all future benefices, and consequently rules out the concession of such a right over a new parish to anyone.[17] If a shortage of qualified priests would warrant the assigning of a religious as priest in charge of a parish either temporarily or for an indefinite period, there would be no need for an indult so long as there is no

---

[12] *De Paroecia*, p. 24.

[13] *Jus Canonicum*, II, 163.

[14] Conc. Trident., sess. XXI, *de ref.*, c. 4; cf. Schmalzgrueber, Lib. III, tit. 48, n. 20.

[15] Canon 1427, § 5. "Divisa paroecia quae ad aliquam religionem iure spectat, vicaria perpetua aut paroecia noviter erecta non est religiosa; . . ."

[16] S.C.C., *Brixinen.*, 16 febr. 1743—*Thesaurus*, XII (1743), 37, 55, 103; Leo XIII, const. *Romanos Pontifices*, 8 maii 1881, nn. 15 and 16—*Fontes*, n. 582. A later decree of the Sacred Congregation of the Council denied an appeal made by the Augustinians against the erection as a secular one of a parish divided from one under their care.—S.C.C., *Ianuen., Dismembrationis*, 25 ian. 1879—*Thesaurus*, CXXXVIII (1879), 56-65.

[17] Canon 1427, § 5; S.C.C., *Brixinen.*—*loc. cit.*

union of the parish with a religious institute. But if the situation was such that only through a union of one type or another the particular needs of the parish could be met, then for the division of such a parish an indult must be secured from the Holy See.[18]

Noteworthy here is the fact that parishes united *plenissimo iure* to an independent abbacy are subject to the jurisdiction of the abbot, who exercises ordinary power over them, and consequently has the power to divide them under the same circumstances which permit other ordinaries to divide parishes.[19]

The formalities prescribed by law for the division of parishes must be employed when a religious parish is concerned, with no exceptions whatsoever. Additional formalities have been suggested, such as the notification of the Holy See by the ordinary regarding the new boundaries of the religious parish.[20] Augustine argued that this is a pertinent formality because "the boundaries of every religious parish are accepted and sanctioned by the Holy See."[21] The Code is silent on this point, but the very fact that ordinaries are empowered by the law to divide these parishes indicates that their decision in regard to the new boundaries is warranted if all the usual prescribed formalities are fulfilled, and that hence a valid and licit division of a religious parish can be accomplished without this notification. If the religious institute believes itself to be the victim of injustice, recourse is open to it.

ARTICLE 2. DIVISION OF NATIONAL PARISHES

Because special regulations govern the establishment and modification of all non-territorial parishes, a particular treatment must be accorded to the question of the division of parishes as it refers to national parishes.[22] "National" parishes will be considered here in the widely used and commonly accepted sense of special par-

[18] Canons 1423, § 2, and 452.

[19] Canon 319. Cf. Wernz-Vidal, *Ius Canonicum,* II, n. 154.

[20] Augustine, *A Commentary on Canon Law,* VI, 509.

[21] *Loc. cit.*

[22] Canon 216, § 4.—Non possunt sine speciali apostolico indulto constitui paroeciae pro diversitate sermonis seu nationis fidelium in eadem civitate vel territorio degentium, nec paroeciae mere familiares aut personales; ad constitutas autem quod attinet, nihil innovandum, inconsulta Apostolica Sede.

ishes distinct by reason of language or national origin. The basic principle used in the law itself, and consequently the conclusions to be derived, will apply to all parishes established on a basis other than a territorial one.

Before the Code the local ordinary was the sole authority besides the Holy See who could establish canonically a national parish with full parochial rights.[23] Ordinaries, then, determined "whether a parish was to be purely personal, that is, for a people of a certain language or nationality, or whether it was to be a mixed personal parish, that is, for the people of a certain language or nationality within definite or approximate limits."[24] Generally taken, before the Code, national parishes in this country had been founded for the people of a certain language. Some, however, had been established for minority groups, people who did not speak English but who were not numerically large enough to support a parish of their own. In this latter case, ordinaries erected territorial parishes, at the same time directing that the minority group in the particular locality be under the jurisdiction of the pastor of a territorial parish, even though this group lived outside the territorial limits of this parish.[25] At the present that would not be considered a national parish in the strict sense, but because the national element is the basis of their subjection to the pastor, there would be required an indult of the Holy See before the parish could be modified—"nihil innovandum inconsulta Apostolica Sede."[26]

Most important for the purpose of this work is the fact that a parish had to be canonically established by the ordinary as such to become a true national parish.[27] Consequently, if national parishes have been lawfully established, they have all the parochial rights that by law are granted to territorial parishes, restricted only according to the principle of personal parishes, and are to be considered as benefices.[28]

---

[23] Augustine, *The Canonical and Civil Status of Catholic Parishes,* p. 77.

[24] Ciesluk, *National Parishes in the United States,* p. 58.

[25] Ciesluk, *op. cit.,* p. 60.

[26] Canon 216, § 4.

[27] Augustine, *The Canonical and Civil Status of Catholic Parishes,* p. 77; Ciesluk, *op. cit.,* p. 78.

[28] Ciesluk, *op. cit.,* pp. 65-68.

The law concerning benefices, then, would apply in the matter of dividing such parishes were there no special regulations indicated in the law itself. The Holy See deems it necessary to examine each case on its merits and to ascertain the most effective policy when a division, or any other form of modification, is considered by the ordinary as necessary or useful. The power to establish or to divide national parishes is not withdrawn from ordinaries, but the exercise of that power is withdrawn—he may act only after he has received a special indult from the Holy See.[29]

When to meet the needs of the people, a division of national parishes is adjudged the only alternative by the ordinary, three fundamental elements must be considered, namely, the parish itself, the consultations with the Holy See, and the contemplated division.

From the wording of the canon, "*ad constitutas autem quod attinet, nihil innovandum, inconsulta Apostolica Sede,*" it is evident that the law which prohibits a "change of status affects only those parishes that have been established and recognized as national parishes with their own proper pastor."[30] The fact of such an effected establishment may be ascertained from the official documents by means of which the parish was erected, or in the absence of these, from other reliable authentic sources of proof. If investigation demonstrates that the parish is truly a national parish, the contemplated division must be referred to the Holy See. In this instance the Sacred Congregation of the Council is competent.[31]

Consultation with the Holy See is demanded by the law when any change in the status of a national parish is being considered. The question as to the invalidity of a division undertaken without such consultation is controverted. The canon requiring the counsel of others for the validity of an act[32] is not sufficiently clear, and authors are divided in their opinion. Those commentators who hold the necessity of seeking counsel to be a fact relevant to

[29] Cf. *ER*, LX (1918), 691.

[30] Ciesluk, *op. cit.*, p. 91.

[31] Pius X, const. *Sapienti consilio*, 29 iun. 1908—*AAS*, I (1909), 11; canon 250.

[32] Canon 105, 1°.

validity follow a strict interpretation of the canon according to the text and context.[33]

Vermeersch-Creusen[34] and others[35] maintain that the words of the law are not clear, and that consequently the consultation is not necessarily required for validity. The invalidity of a division attempted without consultation cannot be insisted upon, as Coronata states,[36] since canon 105, 1°, seems to refer only to those cases in which the law requires the consent or counsel for a valid act.

However, canon 216, § 4, has reference to a consultation between a subordinate, the bishop, with his superior, the Holy See, and the words of the canon could be construed as requiring consent.[37] It is indeed not unlikely that the requisite consultation with a superior has a favored position as compared with the required consultation with subordinates, and that, although the neglect of the latter under canon 105, 1° might not render an act invalid, yet the neglect of consultation with the Holy See would. There is a great difference, however, between a consultation with a superior and the consent of the superior, and such consultation does not necessarily imply that an act performed without consultation would be invalid. A number of canons requiring consultation with the ordinary,[38] and even his permission,[39] seem to indicate this.

When the law reserves to the Holy See the exclusive power for some action, there is employed a definitely more restrictive terminology than that which occurs in Canon 216, § 4.[40] For example,

---

[33] Maroto, *Institutiones Iuris Canonici* (2 vols., Vol. I, 3. ed., Romae, 1919-1921), I, n. 47; Ferreres, *Institutiones Canonicae* (2. ed., 2 vols., Barcinone, 1920), I, n. 229; Beste, *Introductio in Codicem,* p. 162; Coronata, *Institutiones Iuris Canonici,* I, n. 153, nota 8.

[34] *Epitome,* I, n. 229.

[35] Bouuaert-Simenon, *Manuale Juris Canonici* (3 vols., Vols. I and III, 3. ed., Vol. II, 1. ed., Gandae et Leodii: Dessain, 1930-1931), I, n. 259; Vromant, "De Actibus Personae Moralis Collegials ac Superioris"—*Ephemerides Theologicae Lovaniensis* (Lovanii-Brugis, 1924-), VII (1930), 681.

[36] *Institutones Iuris Canonici,* I, n. 153.

[37] Cf. Reiffenstuel, Lib. III, tit. X, n. 4, for the older concept.

[38] Canons 137; 767; 919; 1023, § 3; 1063, § 2; 1065, § 2; 1066.

[39] Canon 1091.

[40] Cf. canons 215, § 1; 494, § 1; 782, § 2; 913, § 1; 1257.

canon 331, § 3, restricts judgment as to the fitness of candidates for the episcopacy *"ad Apostolicam Sedem unice."* An action performed contrary to such prescriptions would be invalid. Sometimes the law emphasizes pointedly that an action undertaken without the permission of the Holy See is invalid or illicit.[41] At other times the law requires consultation rather than permission.[42]

Moreover, authors agree generally that bishops may establish validly a religious congregation even apart from the consultation with the Holy See which the law requires.[43] Likewise, the ordinary can validly, though at the same time but illicitly, withdraw jurisdiction from *all* the confessors of a religious house.[44] Hence, if the ordinary can act validly, though not licitly, when consultation with the Holy See is required in matters in which he has ordinary power, it seems logical to conclude that a consultation with the Holy See is not required for the validity of the division of a national parish. On the other hand, if insufficient reasons appear to have been the basis for the division, recourse to the Sacred Congregation should be made. In this way the Holy See would have ample opportunity to examine the case, and the neglected consultation could be supplied after the fact.

When does the division of a national parish become necessary or advisable? Ordinarily a national parish does not suddenly become a parish of people speaking the language and accepting the customs of the country in which they now live. The gradual intermingling with the native population, intermarriage, joint education with those of the dominant nationality, and similar circumstances break down the barriers that first called for the erection of a national parish. The dominant native language and customs effect a factual change in public relations and in the home. A corresponding juridical change cannot be viewed with disfavor on the basis of religion or reason.[45]

The new generation which develops becomes by degrees a part of the native population, imbued with its language and culture,

---

[41] Canons 534, § 1; 955, § 2; 978, § 3; 1073; 1147, § 1.

[42] Canons 217, § 2; 492, § 1; 517, § 2; 888, § 3.

[43] Canon 492, § 1; Coronata, *Institutiones Iuris Canonici,* I, n. 543.

[44] Canon 880, § 3; Vermeersch-Creusen, *Epitome,* II, n. 150.

[45] Ciesluk, *National Parishes in the United States,* p. 94.

and differing from parents and grandparents in nationality. For the "American nationality" is no less a real one than that of the Irish, British, Polish, or Italian nationality of the forefathers of those who are now American citizens.[46] In the face of such a development there no longer exists a difference of language or nationality, and ordinaries may seek to suppress the parish, to convert it into a territorial one, or to divide it in such a way as to leave a portion of it as a national parish for those of the older generation. Any of these processes requires consultation with the Holy See.[47]

Consultation is required also when the growth of a national parish warrants its division into two such parishes. In this instance most probably it would be sufficient to petition for a permission to establish a new national parish, if at the same time the circumstances which prompt such action be duly indicated in the petition. When this type of division has been effected it is advisable, both for reasons of proper administration and from the standpoint of the civil law, to define the boundaries within which each parish is contained.[48]

Apparently it is not necessary to consult with the Holy See in cases which involve a decision to define boundaries between national parishes heretofore not clearly defined.[49] Neither is there need for approaching the Holy See when English is introduced, in addition to the foreign idiom, in sermons, in the teaching of catechism, and in the hearing of confessions, provided that the spiritual welfare of those who use the other language suffers no neglect.[50]

---

[46] Eppstein, *The Catholic Tradition of the Law of Nations* (London: Burns, Oates and Washbourne, Ltd., 1935), p. 384.

[47] Canon 1422 reserves to the Holy See the suppression or the extinctive union of all benefices, whereas canon 216, § 4, simply demands a consultation with the Holy See if any changes of status in national parishes is to be lawfully undertaken.

[48] Ciesluk, *National Parishes in the United States*, p. 95.

[49] S.R.R., *in causa Annecien., Finium Parochialium*, 5 febr., 1918, *coram R.P.D. Joanne Prior*, Dec. III—S.R.R., *Decisiones*, X (1918), 18-26.

[50] Studies and Conferences, "Pastor Halloft and Foreign-born Catholics"—*ER*, LXXII (1925), 85.

It has come to be generally held that parishes for colored people can be called, in certain circumstances, national parishes. The mind of the Church, of course, is that there is no racial distinction to be made in the bond of faith, but in the United States, which is not a Catholic country, there is a definite racial problem. If the Church has found it necessary to establish separate churches for the colored, it is only because her purpose and that of her people will be better served in that way. Since the normal reason for establishing national parishes is the diversity of language, colored parishes would be more appropriately classified under personal parishes, either strictly so or cumulatively territorial.[51] Nationality can be considered from the standpoint of political unity or as a characteristic of a people of a common origin, and under the latter division colored parishes certainly can be included.[52]

If a parish for colored people exists coextensively with one territorial parish, or embraces people in several territorial parishes, a division of it would follow the rules prescribed for the division of national parishes. If, on the other hand, a canonical territorial parish exists in an entirely colored district, the regulations discussed previously concerning territorial division would hold, since it could not claim to be a national parish in that event. The guiding principle which could serve as a norm for determining the canonical status of colored parishes seems to be this: Whenever a parish church has been established for the use of a colored congregation, excluding all others living within the same territory or district, then it must be considered a personal parish, subject to modification only by virtue of an apostolic indult.[53]

The same principle would apply to the division of parishes which have been established for other racial groups, such as the Indians and Chinese.[54]

---

[51] Bastnagel, "Is a Parish for Colored People a 'National' Parish?"—*ER,* CVIII (1943), 383; Cappello, *Summa Iuris Canonici,* II, n. 488. Connolly maintains that colored parishes are included under the ruling of canon 216, § 4, not in consequence of their personal character in the strict sense, but because of their non-territorial character.—*The Canonical Erection of Parishes,* p. 107.

[52] Ciesluk, *National Parishes in the United States,* p. 100.

[53] Cf. Bastnagel, "Is a Parish for Colored People a 'National' Parish"—*ER,* CVIII (1943), 384.

[54] Connolly, *The Canonical Erection of Parishes,* p. 107.

ARTICLE 3. DIVISION OF ORIENTAL PARISHES IN THE UNITED STATES

In the United States the presence of large numbers of Catholics of Oriental rites is of comparatively recent development. Greek-Ruthenians first began to come to this country in large numbers about the year 1879. By 1910 there were an estimated 371,500 Ruthenians in the United States.[55] Until 1912, when a separate diocese for the Greek-Ruthenians in the United States was created, they were dependent on Latin ordinaries. At that time the Ruthenian bishop received full jurisdiction over the faithful and the clergy of the Greek-Ruthenian rite, and became directly subject to the Holy See.[56] Later, another diocese was created, one with headquarters in Homestead, Pa., and the other in Philadelphia.[57]

Ruthenian ordinaries now exercise jurisdiction similar to that of Latin ordinaries, except that it is both personal and territorial, with the personal element depending on the native land of the people.[58] Consequently, the jurisdiction of Ruthenian ordinaries is territorially coextensive with that of the Latin bishops of this country. When a group of Ruthenians, sufficiently large to support a parish or a mission, settles in a Latin diocese in which there is no Ruthenian church, the Latin ordinary must notify the Ruthenian ordinary or the Sacred Oriental Congregation through the Apostolic Delegate.[59]

If a priest is sent to supply the spiritual needs of the people, a church must be erected or given over to him. This implies that the Latin ordinary will assign a certain location on which a church can be built, if there is no church available for the use of the people concerned. In the event that the number of Ruthenians would grow beyond the capacity of the church, or if other canonical reasons, such as the difficulty of approach because of great

---

[55] *Statistica con Cenni Storici della Gerarchia e dei Fideli di Rito Orientale* (Roma: Tipografia Poliglotta Vaticana, 1932), p. 213.

[56] Cf. "Extension of Jurisdiction of the Ruthenian Bishop for the United States"—*ER*, XLIX (1913), 473.

[57] Bouscaren, *The Canon Law Digest*, I, 7.

[58] S.C. pro Ecclesia Orientali, decr. *Cum data fuerit*, 1 mart. 1929—*AAS*, XXI (1929), 152-159.

[59] Bouscaren, *op. cit.*, I, 19.

distance, would exist and indicate the need for a division of the parish into another Ruthenian parish, then it seems necessary that a consultation between the two ordinaries should take place for the purpose of determining the most effective means of solving the problem. In the absence of any prescriptions in the law itself this appears to be the most equitable procedure, especially in view of the overlapping territorial jurisdictions.

Inasmuch as the faithful concerned are entirely subject to the Ruthenian ordinary, the ordinance regarding the number of the faithful to be assigned to the new parish regarding the endowment to be guaranteed or assured, and regarding the size of the physical plant would be left entirely to the Ruthenian ordinary. The Latin bishop would be most concerned about the possible infringements on the rights of already existing parishes under his jurisdiction, and would have a right to protect his interests in the discussion with the other ordinary. Any controversies between the two ordinaries are to be referred to the Sacred Oriental Congregation.[60]

All other Orientals, the Maronites, Melchites, Italo-Greeks, Rumanians, Syrians, Armenians, and Chaldeans, have been placed under the jurisdiction of the respective Latin ordinaries in whose dioceses they have a domicile or quasi-domicile.[61] They retain their rite,[62] and are held to the prescriptions of the law of their own discipline, unless they have been exempted by the Code or by special provisions of the Holy See.[63]

Latin ordinaries may establish separate churches and missions for them and divide or otherwise modify already established parishes, according to the law of the Code.[64] Consequently, the Latin ordinaries will apply the same rules to Oriental parishes, other than Ruthenian parishes, which govern the division of territorial parishes in their dioceses.

[60] Bouscaren, *The Canon Law Digest,* I, 9.

[61] Cf. S.C. de Prop. Fide pro Neg. R.O., 17 aug. 1914—*AAS,* VI (1914), 458; Duskie, *The Canonical Status of Oriental Catholics in the United States,* p. 35.

[62] Leo XIII, const. *"Orientalium dignitas,"* 20 nov. 1894, 9—*Fontes,* n. 627.

[63] Canon 1.

[64] The restrictions of canon 216, § 4, do not apply to parishes of Orientals. Cf. Maroto, *Institutiones Iuris Canonici,* II, n. 771; Coronata, *Institutiones Iuris Canonici,* I, n. 309, p. 367 in nota 4.

CONCLUSIONS

1. Legislation concerning the division of parishes has always prescribed that canonical causes be present before a division could be validly undertaken.

2. Although the Council of Trent enumerated but one canonical cause for a division of parishes, namely the great difficulty of approach to the parish church, the jurisprudence of the Roman Congregations supported a second cause, the excessive number of parishioners. This second cause is now recognized as a matter of law. The law leaves the determination of the existence of a cause to the discretion of the ordinary.

3. The better opinion is that when the diocese will benefit from the division of a parish, vicars capitular or administrators may divide a parish.

4. Consultation with the cathedral chapter or the diocesan consultors is probably necessary for the validity of the division of a parish.

5. An essential formality before the division may be effected is the guarantee of an adequate source of revenue. In the United States, ordinaries can divide parishes solely on the basis of anticipated revenue.

6. The documents testifying to the division and to the establishment of the new parish should be preserved in both the diocesan and the parish archives.

7. Religious parishes are considered ex aequo in law to parishes under the care of diocesan priests in matters pertaining to their division, no additional formalities being required.

8. A canonically established national parish, including colored parishes, cannot be divided without an indult from the Holy See.

9. The division of Greek-Ruthenian parishes in the United States requires a consultation between the Latin and Ruthenian ordinaries. Other Oriental parishes follow the law of the Code.

BIBLIOGRAPHY

SOURCES

Acta Apostolicae Sedis, Commentarium Officiale, Romae, 1909-.

Acta Sanctae Sedis, 41 vols., Romae, 1865-1908.

Acta et Decreta Concilii Plenarii Baltimorensis Tertii, Baltimorae, 1886.

Bouscaren, T. Lincoln, *The Canon Law Digest,* 2 vols., Milwaukee: Bruce, 1934, 1943.

Bullarum Diplomatum et Privilegiorum Sanctorum Romanorum Pontificum Taurinensis Editio, 25 vols., Augustae Taurinorum, 1857-1872.

Bullarum Pontificium Sacrae Congregationis de Propaganda Fide, ed. S. Bayer, 7 vols. et Index, Romae, 1839-1858.

Codex Iuris Canonici Pii X Pontificis Maximi iussu digestus Benedicti Papae XV Auctoritate promulgatus, Praefatione, Fontium annotatione et Indice Analytico-Alphabetico ab Eño Petro Card. Gasparri Auctus, Romae: Typis Polyglottis Vaticanis, 1917.

Codicis Iuris Canonici Fontes cura Eñi Petri Card. Gasparri editi, 9 vols., Romae (postea Civitate Vaticana): Typis Polyglottis Vaticanis, 1923-1939. (Vols. VII-IX, ed. cura et studio Eñi Iustiniani Serédi.)

Collectanea S. Congregationis de Propaganda Fide, 2 vols., Romae: Typographia Polyglotta, S.C. de Propaganda Fide, 1907.

Concilium Tridentinum, Diariorum, Actorum, Epistularum, Tractatuum, Nova Collectio. Edidit Societas Goerresiana. 13 vols., Friburgi Brisgoviae: B. Herder, 1901-1938.

Corpus Iuris Canonici, ed. Lipsiensis II (Richter-Friedberg), 2 vols., Lipsiae, 1879-1881.

Corpus Iuris Civilis, 3 vols., Berolini, 1928-1929. *Institutiones,* quas recognovit P. Krueger; *Digesta,* quae recognovit T. Mommsen et retractavit P. Krueger; *Codex Iustinianus,* quem recognovit et retractavit P. Krueger; *Novellae,* quas recognovit R. Schoell et absolvit G. Kroll.

Decisiones S. Romanae Rotae coram Alexandro Falconerio, 5 vols., Romae, 1727-1730.

Decretales D. Gregorii Papae IX, suae integritati, una cum glossis restitutae, Romae, 1582.

Decretum Gratiani, emendatum et notationibus illustratum, una cum glossis, 2 vols., Romae, 1582.

Denzinger, Heinrich, Bannwart, Clemens, et Umberg, Johannes, *Enchiridion Symbolorum, Definitionum, et Declarationum de Rebus Fidei et Morum,* 21-23. ed. Friburgi Brisgoviae: Herder & Co., 1937.

Hardouin, Jean, *Acta Conciliorum et Epistolae Decretales ac Constituiones Summorum Pontificium,* 12 vols., Parisiis, 1714-1715.

Jaffé, Philippus, *Regesta Pontificum Romanorum ab condita Ecclesia ad annum post Christum natum MCXCVIII* correctam et auctam auspiciis Wattenbach curaverunt S. Loewenfeld, F. Kaltenbrunner, G. Ewald (2. ed.) 2 vols. in 1, Lipsiae, 1885-1888.

Mansi, J. D., *Sacrorum Conciliorum Nova et Amplissima Collection,* 53 vols. in 60, Parisiis, 1901-1927.

Monumenta Germaniae Historica, 188 vols., incomplete, Hanoverae, 1826- ; *Leges,* 5 vols., ed. Georgius Pertz, 1875-1889.

Pallottini, S., *Collectio omnium conclusionum et resolutionum quae in causis propositis apud Sacram Congregationem Cardinalium S. Concilii Tridentini interpretum prodierunt ab eius institutione anno MDLXIV ad annum MDCCCLX distinctis titulis alphabetico ordine per materias digesta,* 18 vols., Romae, 1868-1895.

Potthast, Augustus, *Regesta Pontificum Romanorum inde ab anno post Christum natum MCXCVIII ad annum MCCCIV,* 2 vols., Berolini, 1874-1875.

Schroeder, H. J., *Canons and Decrees of the Council of Trent,* St. Louis: B. Herder & Co., 1941.

Sacrae Romanae Rotae Decisiones seu Sententiae, 31 vols., Romae: Typis Vaticanis, 1912-1948. *Decisiones Recentiores,* 19 partes in 25 vols., Francofurti, Aurelianae, Romae, 1623-1703.

Statistica con Cenni della Gerarchia e dei Fedeli di Rito Orientale, Romae: Tipografia Poliglotta Vaticana, 1932.

Statuta Archidioecesis Sancti Francisci Lata ac Promulgata ab Excellentissimo ac Reverendissimo Joanne J. Mitty Archiepiscopo Sancti Francisci in Synodo Dioecesana Secunda, San Francisco: The Monitor Publishing Co., 1936.

Thesaurus Resolutionum Sacrae Congregationis Concilii, 167 vols., Romae, 1708-1908.

Reference Works

Augustine, Charles, *A Commentary on the New Code of Canon Law,* 3. ed., 8 vols., St. Louis: Herder & Co., 1910-1931; Vol. VI, 3. ed., 1931.

———, *The Canonical and Civil Status of Parishes in the United States,* St. Louis, 1926.

Ayrinhac, H. A., *Administrative Legislation in the New Code of Canon Law,* New York: Longmans, Green and Co., 1923.

———, *Constitution of the Church in the New Code of Canon Law,* New York: Benziger, 1925.

———, *General Legislation in the New Code of Canon Law,* New York: Longmans, Green and Co., 1923.

Barbosa, Augustinus, *Collectanea Doctorum in varia Concilii Tridentini Decreta et Canones,* Lugduni, 1658.

———, *De officio et potestate Episcopi,* 2 vols., Romae, 1656.

———, *Iuris Ecclesiastici Universi Libri Tres,* 3 vols., Lugduni, 1650.

Bargilliat, M., *Praelectiones Juris Canonici,* 36. ed., 2 vols., Parisiis, 1923.

Bastnagel, Clement, *The Appointment of Parochial Adjutants and Assistants,* The Catholic University of America Canon Law Studies, n. 58, Washington, D. C.: The Catholic University of America, 1930.

Berutti, C., *Institutiones Iuris Canonici,* 6 vols., Vol. II, Pars I, 1943; Vol. IV, 1940; Romae, Marietti.

Beste, Udalricus, *Introductio in Codicem,* 2. ed., Collegeville, Minn.,: St. John's Abbey Press, 1944.

Bouix, Dominicus, *Tractatus de Parocho,* 3. ed., Parisiis, 1880.

Brown, Brendan F., *The Canonical Juristic Personality with Special Reference to its Status in the United States of America,* The Catholic University of America Canon Law Studies, n. 38, Washington, D. C.: The Catholic University of America, 1927.

Cappello, Felix M., *De Curia Romana,* 2 vols., Romae, 1911.

———, *Summa Iuris Canonici,* 3 vols., Vol. I and Vol. II, 4. ed., Romae: Apud Aedes Universitatis Gregorianae, 1945; Vol. III, ed. altera, 1940.

Cicognani, Amleto, *Canon Law,* 2. ed., revised, Westminster, Md.,: Newman Bookshop, 1946.

Ciesluk, Joseph E., *National Parishes in the United States,* The Catholic University of America Canon Law Studies, n. 190, The Catholic University of America Press, 1944.

Claeys Bouuaert, F.-Simenon, G., *Manuale Juris Canonici,* 3 vols., Vol. I and Vol. III, 3. ed., Vol. II, 1. ed., Gandae et Leodii: Dessain, 1930-1931.

Cocchi, Guidus, *Commentarium in Codicem Iuris Canonici,* 8 vols. in 5, Vol. V (Lib. III, *De Rebus;* Pars II, *De Locis et Temporibus sacris;* Pars III, *De Cultu divino*), 4. ed., Taurinorum Augustae: Marietti, 1938.

Connolly, Nicholas P., *The Canonical Erection of Parishes,* The Catholic University of America Canon Law Studies, n. 114, Washington, D. C.: The Catholic University of America, 1938.

Coronata, Mattheus Conte A., *Institutiones Iuris Canonici,* 5 vols., Vols. I-II, 2. ed., 1939; Vols. III-V, 1933-1936, Taurini, Marietti.

De Luca, Ioannes Card., *Theatrum Veritatis et Iustitiae,* 16 vols., Coloniae Agrippinae, 1576.

De Meester, A., *Juris Canonici et Juris Canonico-Civilis Compendium,* nova editio, 3 vols. in 4, Brugis: Descleé, De Brouwer, 1921-1928.

Doheny, William J., *Church Property: Modes of Acquisition,* The Catholic University of America Canon Law Studies, n. 41, Washington, D. C.: The Catholic University of America, 1927.

Duskie, John, *The Canonical Status of Oriental Catholics in the United States,* The Catholic University of America Canon Law Studies, n. 48, Washington, D. C.: The Catholic University of America, 1928.

Eppstein, John, *The Catholic Tradition of the Law of Nations*, London: Burns, Oates and Washbourne, Ltd., 1935.

Fagnanus, Prosper, *Commentaria super Quin que Libros Decretalium*, 4 vols., Venetiis, 1697.

Fanfani, P. Ludovicus, *De Iure Parochorum*, ed. altera, Taurini-Romae: Marietti, 1936.

Ferraris, Lucius, *Bibliotheca Canonica, Iuridica, Moralis, Theologica necnon Ascetica, Polemica, Rubricistica, Historica*, 9 vols., Romae, 1885-1899.

Ferreres, Joannes B., *Institutiones Canonicae*, 2. ed., 2 vols., Barcinone, 1920.

Ferry, William A., *Stole Fees*, The Catholic University of America Canon Law Studies, n. 59, Washington, D. C.: The Catholic University of America, 1930.

Funk, F. X., *Lehrbuch der Kirchengeschichte*, 2 vols., increased and revised by Karl Behlmeyer, Paderborn, 1921.

Garcia, Nicolaus, *De Beneficiis Ecclesiasticis Amplissimus et Doctissimus Tractatus*, Venetiis, 1618.

Godfrey, John, *The Right of Patronage according to the Code of Canon Law*, The Catholic University of America Canon Law Studies, n. 21, Washington, D. C.: The Catholic University of America, 1924.

Gonzalez-Tellez, Emmanuel, *Commentaria Perpetua in Singulos Textus Quinque Librorum Decretalium Gregorii* IX, 5 vols., Maceratae, 1761.

Hostiensis, Cardinalis (Henricus de Segusia), *In Quinque Decretalium Libros Commentaria*, 5 vols. in 3, Venetiis, 1581.

Jaeger, Leo A., *The Administration of Vacant and Quasi-Vacant Dioceses in the United States*, The Catholic University of America Canon Law Studies, n. 81, Washington, D. C.: The Catholic University of America, 1932.

Kremer, Michael N., *Church Support in the United States*, The Catholic University of America Canon Law Studies, n. 61, Washington, D. C.: The Catholic University of America, 1930.

Laurentius, Joseph, *Institutiones Juris Canonici*, Friburgi Brisgoviae, 1903.

Leage, R. W., *Roman Private Law*, London: MacMillan, 1932.

Leurenius, Petrus, *Forum Beneficiale*, 2 vols., Venetiis, 1742.

McClunn, Justin D., *Administrative Recourse*, The Catholic University of America Canon Law Studies, n. 240, Washington, D. C.: The Catholic University of America Press, 1946.

Maroto, Philippus, *Institutiones Iuris Canonici*, Vol. I, 3. ed., 2 vols., Romae, 1919-1921.

Monacellus, Franciscus, *Formularium Legale Practicum Fori Ecclesiastici*, 3. ed., 4 vols. in 3, Romae, 1844.

Mothon, Joseph P., *Institutions Canoniques*, 3 vols., Paris, 1922-1924.

Mundy, Thomas M., *The Union of Parishes*, The Catholic University of America Canon Law Studies, n. 204, Washington, D. C.: The Catholic University of America Press, 1945.

Ojetti, Benedictus, *Commentarium in Codicem Iuris Canonici,* 4 vols., Romae: Universitas Gregoriana, 1927-1931.

——, *Synopsis Rerum Moralium et Iuris Pontificii,* Romae, 1899.

Panormitanus, Abbas (Nicholaus de Tudeschis), *Commentaria in Quinque Libros Decretalium,* 5 vols. in 8, Venetiis, 1588.

Petrani, Alexius, *De Relatione Iuridica inter Diversos Ritus in Ecclesia Catholica,* Taurini: Marietti, 1930.

Pirhing, Enricus, *Jus Canonicum in V Libros Decretalium distributum,* 5 vols., Venetiis, 1659-1677.

Pistocchi, Marius, *De Re Beneficiali iuxta Canones,* Taurini: Marietti, 1928.

Pyrrhus, Corradus, *Praxis Beneficiaria,* Venetiis, 1735.

Reiffenstuel, Anacletus, *Jus Canonicum Universum,* 5 vols. in 7, Parisiis, 1864-1870.

Rossi, Josephus, *De Paroecia,* Romae: Pustet, 1923.

Schmalzgrueber, Franciscus, *Jus Ecclesiasticum Universum,* 5 vols. in 12, Romae, 1843-1845.

Sebastianelli, G., *Praelectiones Iuris Canonici, De Rebus,* Romae, 1905.

Sipos, S., *Enchiridion Iuris Canonici,* 4. ed., Pécs: Ex Typographia "Haladás R.T.," 1940.

Thomassinus, Ludovicus, *Vetus et Nova Ecclesiae Disciplina,* 3 vols., Parisiis, 1688.

Van Hove, *Prolegomena ad Codicem Iuris Canonici,* ed. altera, Mechliniae et Romae: Dessain, 1945.

Vermeersch, A.-Creusen, J., *Epitome Iuris Canonici,* 6. ed., 3 vols., Mechliniae, Romae: Dessain, 1937-1946.

Wernz, F. X., *Jus Decretalium,* 2. ed., 6 vols., Romae et Prati, 1898-1905.

Wernz, F.-Vidal, P., *Ius Canonicum ad Codicis Normam Exactum,* 7 toms. in 8 vols., Romae: Apud Aedes Universitatis Gregorianae, 1923-1938; Tom. II, De Personis, 2. ed., 1928; Tom. V, *Jus Matrimoniale,* 2. ed., 1928.

Woywod, Stanislaus, *A Practical Commentary on the Code of Canon Law,* 2 vols., ninth printing, edited by C. S. Smith, New York: J. Wagner, Inc.; London: Herder, 1945.

Periodicals

American Ecclesiastical Review, The, Vols. I-XXXII, Philadelphia, 1889-1905; *The Ecclesiastical Review,* Vols. XXXIII-CIX, Philadelphia, 1905-1943; from 1944: *The American Ecclesiastical Review,* Vol. CX, Washington, D. C., 1944-

Analecta Ecclesiastica, Paris, 1893-1911.

Apollinaris, Romae, 1928-

Ephemerides Theologicae Lovanienses, Lovanii-Brugis, 1924-

Jurist, The, Washington, D. C.: The Catholic University of America, 1941-

Monitore Ecclesiastica, II, Romae, 1876-
Nouvelle Revue Théologique, Tournai, 1869-
Jus Pontificium, Romae, 1921-1940.

Articles

Bastnagel, C., "Is a Parish for Colored People a 'National' Parish?"—*ER,* CVIII (1943), 382-384.

Hannan, J., "The Obligation of Church Support,"—*The Jurist,* I (1941), 343-344.

Marato, P., "Animadversiones,"—*Apollinaris,* VI (1933), 421-431.

Ojetti, B., "In Canonem 105 Codicis Iuris Canonici,"—*Jus Pontificium,* VII (1927), 13-25.

Rucupis E., "The Canonical Formation of Parishes and Missions"—*ER,* LV (1916), 238-250.

Studies and Conferences, "Pastor Halloft and Foreign-born Catholics,"—*ER,* LXXII (1925), 84-87.

Vromant, G., "De Actibus Personae Moralis Collegialis ac Superioris"—*Ephemerides Theologicae Lovaniensis,* VII (1930), 676-688.

ABBREVIATIONS

AAS—*Acta Apostolicae Sedis.*
AER—*American Ecclesiastical Review.*
ASS—*Acta Sanctae Sedis.*
ER—*Ecclesiastical Review.*
Fontes—*Codicis Iuris Canonici Fontes cura . . . Gasparri editi.*
Hardouin—*Acta Conciliorum, etc.*
Mansi—*Sacrorum Conciliorum Nova et Amplissima Collectio.*
MGH—*Monumenta Germaniae Historica.*
S.C.C.—Sacra Congregatio Concilii.
S. C. Consist.—Sacra Congregatio Consistorialis.
S.R.R.—Sacra Romana Rota.

BIOGRAPHICAL NOTE

Edward P. McCaslin was born on December 4, 1915, at Havre, Montana. He attended Holy Angels' Parochial School and Holy Name High School, both in Omaha, Nebraska. He pursued his studies for the priesthood at Conception College, Conception, Missouri, and at the Theological College of the Catholic University of America, Washington, D. C. In 1940 he received the degree of Master of Arts from the School of Philosophy of the Catholic University, and the Licentiate in Sacred Theology in May, 1944, from the School of Sacred Theology of the same University. He was ordained to the sacred priesthood on May 27, 1944. In September of the following year, he enrolled in the School of Canon Law of the Catholic University of America, where he received the Degree of the Baccalaureate in Canon Law in May, 1946, and the Degree of the Licentiate in Canon Law in June, 1947.

ALPHABETICAL INDEX

CANON LAW STUDIES*

1. Freriks, Rev. Celestine A., C.PP.S., J.C.D., Religious Congregations in Their External Relations, 121 pp. 1916.
2. Galliher, Rev. Daniel M., O.P., J.C.D., Canonical Elections, 117 pp., 1917.
3. Borkowski, Rev. Aurelius L., O.F.M., J.C.D., De Confraternibus Ecclesiasticis, 136 pp., 1918.
4. Castillo, Rev. Cayo, J.C.D., Disertacion Historico-Canonica sobre la Potestad del Cabildo en Sede Vacante o Impedida del Vicario Capitular, 99 pp., 1919 (1918).
5. Kubelbeck, Rev. William J., S.T.B., J.C.D., The Sacred Penitentiaria and Its Relation to Faculties of Ordinaries and Priests, 129 pp., 1918.
6. Petrovits, Rev. Joseph, J.C., S.T.D., J.C.D., The New Church Law on Matrimony, X-461 pp., 1919.
7. Hickey, Rev. John J., S.T.B., J.C.D., Irregularities and Simple Impediments in the New Code of Canon Law, 100 pp., 1920.
8. Klekotka, Rev. Peter J., S.T.B., J.C.D., Diocesan Consultors, 179 pp., 1920.
9. Wanenmacher, Rev. Francis, J.C.D., The Evidence in Ecclesiastical Procedure Affecting the Marriage Bond, 1920 (Printed 1935).
10. Golden, Rev. Henry Francis, J.C.D., Parochial Benefices in the New Code, IV-119 pp., 1921 (Printed 1925).
11. Koudelka, Rev. Charles J., J.C.D., Pastors, Their Rights and Duties According to the New Code of Canon Law, 211 pp., 1921.
12. Melo, Rev. Antonius, O.F.M., J.C.D., De Exemptione Regularium, X-188 pp., 1921.
13. Schaaf, Rev. Valentine Theodore, O.F.M., S.T.B., J.C.D., The Cloister, X-180 pp., 1921.
14. Burke, Rev. Thomas Joseph, S.T.D., J.C.D., Competence in Ecclesiastical Tribunals, IV-117 pp., 1922.
15. Leech, Rev. George Leo, J.C.D., A Comparative Study of the Constitution "Apostolicae Sedis" and the "Codex Juris Canonici," 179 pp., 1922.
16. Motry, Rev. Hubert Louis, S.T.D., J.C.D., Diocesan Faculties According to the Code of Canon Law, II-167 pp., 1922.
17. Murphy, Rev. George Lawrence, J.C.D., Delinquencies and Penalties in the Administration and the Reception of the Sacraments, IV-121 pp., 1923.

*All published numbers are available from the Catholic University of America Press, 620 Michigan Avenue, N.E., Washington 17, D. C., except the following: Nos. 1-114 inclusive, 115, 118, 120, 122, 123, 136, 153, 162, 182 and 198. But the following numbers, now reissued, are obtainable from *The Jurist*, The Catholic University of America, Washington 17, D. C., namely: Nos. 5, 7, 11, 17, 18, 19, 26, 28, 30, 31, 34, 42, 44, 51, 52 and 61.

18. O'REILLY, REV. JOHN ANTHONY, S.T.B., J.C.D., Ecclesiastical Sepulture in the New Code of Canon Law, II-129 pp., 1923.
19. MICHALICKA, REV. WENCESLAS CYRILL, O.S.B., J.C.D., Judicial Procedure in Dismissal of Clerical Exempt Religious, 107 pp., 1923.
20. DARGIN, REV. EDWARD VINCENT, S.T.B., J.C.D., Reserved Cases According to the Code of Canon Law, IV-103 pp., 1924.
21. GODFREY, REV. JOHN A., S.T.B., J.C.D., The Right of Patronage According to the Code of Canon Law, 153 pp., 1924.
22. HAGEDORN, REV. FRANCIS EDWARD, J.C.D., General Legislation on Indulgences, II-154 pp., 1924.
23. KING, REV. JAMES IGNATIUS, J.C.D., The Administration of the Sacraments to Dying Non-Catholics, V-141 pp., 1924.
24. WINSLOW, REV. FRANCIS JOSEPH, O.F.M., J.C.D., Vicars and Prefects Apostolic, IV-149 pp., 1924.
25. CORREA, REV. JOSE SERVELION, S.T.L., J.C.D., La Potestad Legislativa de la Iglesia Catolica, IV-127 pp., 1925.
26. DUGAN, REV. HENRY FRANCIS, A.M., J.C.D., The Judiciary Department of the Diocesan Curia, 87 pp., 1925.
27. KELLER, REV. CHARLES FREDERICK, S.T.B., J.C.D., Mass Stipends, 167 pp., 1925.
28. PASCHANG, REV. JOHN LINUS, J.C.D., The Sacramentals According to the Code of Canon Law, 129 pp., 1925.
29. PIONTEK, REV. CYRILLUS, O.F.M., S.T.B., J.C.D., De Indulto Exclaustrationis necnon Saecularizationis, XIII-289 pp., 1925.
30. KEARNEY, REV. RICHARD JOSEPH, S.T.B., J.C.D., Sponsors at Baptism According to the Code of Canon Law, IV-127 pp., 1925.
31. BARTLETT, REV. CHESTER JOSEPH, A.M., LL.B., J.C.D., The Tenure of Parochial Property in the United States of America, V-108 pp., 1926.
32. KILKER, REV. ADRIAN JEROME, J.C.D., Extreme Unction, V-425 pp., 1926.
33. MCCORMICK, REV. ROBERT EMMETT, J.C.D., Confessors of Religious, VIII-266 pp., 1926.
34. MILLER, REV. NEWTON THOMAS, J.C.D., Founded Masses According to the Code of Canon Law, VII-93 pp., 1926.
35. ROELKER, REV. EDWARD G., S.T.D., J.C.D., Principles of Privilege According to the Code of Canon Law, XI-166 pp., 1926.
36. BAKALARCZYK, REV. RICHARDUS, M.I.C., J.U.D., De Novitiatu, VIII-208 pp., 1927.
37. PIZZUTI, REV. LAWRENCE, O.F.M., J.U.L., De Parochis Religiosis, 1927. (Not Printed.)
38. BLILEY, REV. NICHOLAS MARTIN, O.S.B., J.C.D., Altars According to the Code of Canon Law, XIX-132 pp., 1927.
39. BROWN, MR. BRENDAN FRANCIS, A.B., LL.M., J.U.D., The Canonical Juristic Personality with Special Reference to its Status in the United States of America, V-212 pp., 1927.

40. Cavanaugh, Rev. William Thomas, C.P., J.U.D., The Reservation of the Blessed Sacrament, VIII-101 pp., 1927.
41. Doheny, Rev. William J., C.S.C., A.B., J.C.D., Church Property: Modes of Acquisition, X-118 pp., 1927.
42. Feldhaus, Rev. Aloysius H., C.PP.S., J.C.D., Oratories, IV-141 pp., 1927.
43. Kelly, Rev. James Patrick, A.B., J.C.D., The Jurisdiction of the Simple Confessor, X-208 pp., 1927.
44. Neuberger, Rev. Nicholas J., J.C.D., Canon 6 or the Relation of the Codex Iuris Canonici to the Preceding Legislation, V-95 pp., 1927.
45. O'Keefe, Rev. Gerald Michael, J.C.D., Matrimonial Dispensations, Powers of Bishops, Priests, and Confessors, VIII-232 pp., 1927.
46. Quigley, Rev. Joseph A. M., A.B., J.C.D., Condemned Societies, 139 pp., 1927.
47. Zaplotnik, Rev. Johannes Leo, J.C.D., De Vicariis Foraneis, X-142 pp., 1927.
48. Duskie, Rev. John Aloysius, A.B., J.C.D., The Canonical Status of the Orientals in the United States, VIII-196 pp., 1928.
49. Hyland, Rev. Francis Edward, J.C.D., Excommunication, Its Nature, Historical Development and Effects, VIII-181 pp., 1928.
50. Reimann, Rev. Gerald Joseph, O.M.C., J.C.D., The Third Order Secular of Saint Francis, 201 pp., 1928.
51. Schenk, Rev. Francis J., J.C.D., The Matrimonial Impediments of Mixed Religion and Disparity of Cult, XVI-318 pp., 1929.
52. Coady, Rev. John Joseph, S.T.D., J.U.D., A.M., The Appointment of Pastors, VIII-150 pp., 1929.
53. Kay, Rev. Thomas Henry, J.C.D., Competence in Matrimonial Procedure, VIII-164 pp., 1929.
54. Turner, Rev. Sidney Joseph, C.P., J.U.D., The Vow of Poverty, XLIX-217 pp., 1929.
55. Kearney, Rev. Raymond A., A.B., S.T.D., J.C.D., The Principles of Delegation, VII-149 pp., 1929.
56. Conran, Rev. Edward James, A.B., J.C.D., The Interdict, V-163 pp., 1930.
57. O'Neill, Rev. William H., J.C.D., Papal Rescripts of Favor, VII-218 pp., 1930.
58. Bastnagel, Rev. Clement Vincent, J.U.D., The Appointment of Parochial Adjutants and Assistants, XV-257 pp., 1930.
59. Ferry, Rev. William A., A.B., J.C.D., Stole Fees, V-136 pp., 1930.
60. Costello, Rev. John Michael, A.B., J.C.D., Domicile and Quasi-Domicile, VII-201 pp., 1930.
61. Kremer, Rev. Michael Nicholas, A.B., S.T.B., J.C.D., Church Support in the United States, VI-136 pp., 1930.
62. Angulo, Rev. Luis, C.M., J.C.D., Legislation de la Iglesia sobre la intencion en la application de la Santa Misa, VII-104 pp., 1931.

63. FREY, REV. WOLFGANG NORBERT, O.S.B., A.B., J.C.D., The Act of Religious Profession, VIII-174 pp., 1931.
64. ROBERTS, REV. JAMES BRENDAN, A.B., J.C.D., The Banns of Marriage, XIV-140 pp., 1931.
65. RYDER, REV. RAYMOND ALOYSIUS, A.B., J.C.D., Simony, IX-151 pp., 1931.
66. CAMPAGNA, REV. ANGELO, PH.D., J.U.D., Il Vicario Generale del Vescovo, VII-205, pp., 1931.
67. COX, REV. JOSEPH GODFREY, A.B., J.C.D., The Administration of Seminaries, VI-124 pp., 1931.
68. GREGORY, REV. DONALD J., J.U.D., The Pauline Privilege, XV-165 pp., 1931.
69. DONOHUE, REV. JOHN F., J.C.D., The Impediment of Crime, VII-110 pp., 1931.
70. DOOLEY, REV. EUGENE A., O.M.I., J.C.D., Church Law on Sacred Relics, IX-143 pp., 1931.
71. ORTH, REV. CLEMENT RAYMOND, O.M.C., J.C.D., The Approbation of Religious Institutes, 171 pp., 1931.
72. PERNICONE, REV. JOSEPH M., A.B., J.C.D., The Ecclesiastical Prohibition of Books, XII-267 pp., 1932.
73. CLINTON, REV. CONNELL, A.B., J.C.D., The Paschal Precept, IX-108 pp., 1932.
74. DONNELLY, REV. FRANCIS B., A.M., S.T.L., J.C.D., The Diocesan Synod, VIII-125 pp., 1932.
75. TORRENTE, REV. CAMILO, C.M.F., J.C.D., Las Procesiones Sagradas, V-145 pp., 1932.
76. MURPHY, REV. EDWIN J., C.PP.S., J.C.D., Suspension Ex Informata Conscientia, XI-122 pp., 1932.
77. MACKENZIE, REV. ERIC F., A.M., S.T.L., J.C.D., The Delict of Heresy in its Commission, Penalization, Absolution, VII-124 pp., 1932.
78. LYONS, REV. AVITUS E., S.T.B., J.C.D., The Collegiate Tribunal of First Instance, XI-147 pp., 1932.
79. CONNOLLY, REV. THOMAS A., J.C.D., Appeals, XI-195 pp., 1932.
80. SANGMEISTER, REV. JOSEPH V., A.B., J.C.D., Force and Fear as Precluding Matrimonial Consent, V-211 pp., 1932.
81. JAEGER, REV. LEO A., A.B., J.C.D., The Administration of Vacant and Quasi-Vacant Episcopal Sees in the United States, IX-229 pp., 1932.
82. RIMLINGER, REV. HERBERT T., J.C.D., Error Invalidating Matrimonial Consent, VII-79 pp., 1932.
83. BARRETT, REV. JOHN D. M., S.S., J.C.D., A Comparative Study of the Councils of Baltimore and the Code of Canon Law, IX-223 pp., 1932.
84. CARBERRY, REV. JOHN J., PH.D., S.T.D., J.C.D., The Juridical Form of Marriage, X-177 pp., 1934.
85. DOLAN, REV. JOHN L., A.B., J.C.D., The Defensor Vinculi, XII-157 pp., 1934.

86. HANNAN, REV. JEROME D., A.M., S.T.D., LL.B., J.C.D., The Canon Law of Wills, IX-517 pp., 1934.
87. LEMIEUX, REV. DELISE A., A.M., J.C.D., The Sentence in Ecclesiastical Procedure, IX-131 pp., 1934.
88. O'ROURKE, REV. JAMES J., A.B., J.C.D., Parish Registers, VII-109 pp., 1934.
89. TIMLIN, REV. BARTHOLOMEW, O.F.M., A.M., J.C.D., Conditional Matrimonial Consent, X-381 pp., 1934.
90. WAHL, REV. FRANCIS X., A.B., J.C.D., The Matrimonial Impediments of Consanguinity and Affinity, VI-125 pp., 1934.
91. WHITE, REV. ROBERT J., A.B., LL.B., S.T.B., J.C.D., Canonical Ante-Nuptial Promises and the Civil Law, VI-152 pp., 1934.
92. HERRERA, REV. ANTONIO PARRA, O.C.D., J.C.D., Legislacion Ecclesiastica sobra el Ayuno y la Abstinencia, XI-191 pp., 1935.
93. KENNEDY, REV. EDWIN J., J.C.D., The Special Matrimonial Process in Cases of Evident Nullity, X-165 pp., 1935.
94. MANNING, REV. JOHN J., A.B., J.C.D., Presumption of Law in Matrimonial Procedure, XI-111 pp., 1935.
95. MOEDER, REV. JOHN M., J.C.D., The Proper Bishop for Ordination and Dismissorial Letters, VII-135 pp., 1935.
96. O'MARA, REV. WILLIAM A., A.B., J.C.D., Canonical Causes for Matrimonial Dispensations, IX-155 pp., 1935.
97. REILLY, REV. PETER, J.C.D., Residence of Pastors, IX-81 pp., 1935.
98. SMITH, REV. MARINER T., O.P., S.T.Lr., J.C.D., The Penal Law for Religious, VIII-169 pp., 1935.
99. WHALEN, REV. DONALD W., A.M., J.C.D., The Value of Testimonial Evidence in Matrimonial Procedure, XIII-297 pp., 1935.
100. CLEARY, REV. JOSEPH F., J.C.D., Canonical Limitations on the Alienation of Church Property, VIII-141 pp., 1936.
101. GLYNN, REV. JOHN C., J.C.D., The Promoter of Justice, XX-337 pp., 1936.
102. BRENNAN, REV. JAMES H., S.S., M.A., S.T.B., J.C.D., The Simple Convalidation of Marriage, VI-135 pp., 1937.
103. BRUNINI, REV. JOSEPH BERNARD, J.C.D., The Clerical Obligations of Canons 139 and 142, X-121 pp., 1937.
104. CONNOR, REV. MAURICE, A.B., J.C.D., The Administrative Removal of Pastors, VIII-159 pp., 1937.
105. GUILFOYLE, REV. MERLIN JOSEPH, J.C.D., Custom, XI-144 pp., 1937.
106. HUGHES, REV. JAMES AUSTIN, A.B., A.M., J.C.D., Witnesses in Criminal Trials of Clerics, IX-140 pp., 1937.
107. JANSEN, REV. RAYMOND J., A.B., S.T.L., J.C.D., Canonical Provisions for Catechetical Instruction, VII-153 pp., 1937.
108. KEALY, REV. JOHN JAMES, A.B., J.C.D., The Introductory Libellus in Church Court Procedure, XI-121 pp., 1937.

109. McManus, Rev. James Edward, C.SS.R., J.C.D., The Administration of Temporal Goods in Religious Institutes, XVI-196 pp., 1937.
110. Moriarty, Rev. Eugene James, J.C.D., Oaths in Ecclesiastical Courts, X-115 pp., 1937.
111. Rainer, Reg. Eligius George, C.SS.R., J.C.D., Suspension of Clerics, XVII-249 pp., 1937.
112. Reilly, Rev. Thomas F., C.SS.R., J.C.D., Visitation of Religious, VI-195 pp., 1938.
113. Moriarty, Rev. Francis E., C.SS.R., J.C.D., The Extraordinary Absolution from Censures, XV-334 pp., 1938.
114. Connolly, Rev. Nicholas P., J.C.D., The Canonical Erection of Parishes, X-132 pp., 1938.
115. Donovan, Rev. James Joseph, J.C.D., The Pastor's Obligation in Prenuptial Investigation, XII-322 pp., 1938.
116. Harrigan, Rev. Robert J., M.A., S.T.B., J.C.D., The Radical Sanation of Invalid Marriages, VIII-208 pp., 1938.
117. Boffa, Rev. Conrad Humbert, J.C.D., Canonical Provisions for Catholic Schools, VII-211 pp., 1939.
118. Parsons, Rev. Anscar John, O.M.Cap., J.C.D., Canonical Elections, XII-236 pp., 1939.
119. Reilly, Rev. Edward Michael, A.B., J.C.D., The General Norms of Dispensation, XII-156 pp., 1939.
120. Ryan, Rev. Gerald Aloysius, A.B., J.C.D., Principles of Episcopal Jurisdiction, XII-172 pp., 1939.
121. Burton, Rev. Francis James, C.S.C., A.B., J.C.D., A Commentary on Canon 1125, X-222 pp., 1940.
122. Miaskiewicz, Rev. Francis Sigismund, J.C.D., Supplied Jurisdiction According to Canon 209, XII-340 pp., 1940.
123. Rice, Rev. Patrick William, A.B., J.C.D., Proof of Death in Prenuptial Investigation, VIII-156 pp., 1940.
124. Anglin, Rev. Thomas Francis, M.S., J.C.D., The Eucharistic Fast, VIII-183 pp., 1941.
125. Coleman, Rev. John Jerome, J.C.D., The Minister of Confirmation, VI-153 pp., 1941.
126. Downs, Rev. John Emmanuel, A.B., J.C.D., The Concept of Clerical Immunity, XI-163 pp., 1941.
127. Esswein, Rev. Anthony Albert, J.C.D., Extrajudicial Penal Powers of Ecclesiastical Superiors, X-144 pp., 1941.
128. Farrell, Rev. Benjamin Francis, M.A., S.T.L., J.C.D., The Rights and Duties of the Local Ordinary Regarding Congregations of Women Religious of Pontifical Approval, V-195 pp., 1941.
129. Feeney, Rev. Thomas John, A.B., S.T.L., J.C.D., Restitutio in Integrum, VI-169 pp., 1941.
130. Findlay, Rev. Stephen William, O.S.B., A.B., J.C.D., Canonical Norms Governing the Deposition and Degradation of Clerics, XVII-279 pp., 1941.

131. Goodwine, Rev. John, A.B., S.T.L., J.C.D., The Right of the Church to Acquire Property, VIII-119 pp., 1941.
132. Heston, Rev. Edward Louis, C.S.C., Ph.D., S.T.D., J.C.D., The Alienation of Church Property in the United States, XII-222 pp., 1941.
133. Hogan, Rev. James John, A.B., S.T.L., J.C.D., Judicial Advocates and Procurators, XIII-200 pp., 1941.
134. Kealy, Rev. Thomas M., A.B., Litt.B., J.C.D., Dowry of Women Religious, IX-152 pp., 1941.
135. Keene, Rev. Michael James, O.S.B., J.C.D., Religious Ordinaries and Canon 198, V-164 pp., 1941 (printed 1942).
136. Kerin, Rev. Charles A., S.S., M.A., S.T.B., J.C.D., The Privation of Christian Burial, XVI-279 pp., 1941.
137. Louis, Rev. William Francis, M.A., J.C.D., Diocesan Archives, X-101 pp., 1941.
138. McDevitt, Rev. Gilbert Joseph, A.B., J.C.D., Legitimacy and Legitimation, X-247 pp., 1941.
139. McDonough, Rev. Thomas Joseph, A.B., J.C.D., Apostolic Administrators, X-217 pp., 1941.
140. Meier, Rev. Carl Anthony, A.B., J.C.D., Penal Administrative Procedure Against Negligent Pastors, XI-240 pp., 1941.
141. Schmidt, Rev. John Rogg, A.B., J.C.D., The Principles of Authentic Interpretation in Canon 17 of the Code of Canon Law, XII-331 pp., 1941.
142. Slafkosky, Rev. Andrew Leonard, A.B., J.C.D., The Canonical Episcopal Visitation of the Diocese, X-197 pp., 1941.
143. Swoboda, Rev. Innocent Robert, O.F.M., J.C.D., Ignorance in Relation to the Imputability of Delicts, IX-271 pp., 1941.
144. Dubé, Rev. Arthur Joseph, A.B., J.C.D., The General Principles for the Reckoning of Time in Canon Law, VIII-299 pp., 1941.
145. McBride, Rev. James T., A.B., J.C.D., Incardination and Excardination of Seculars, XX-585 pp., 1941.
146. Król, Rev. John T., J.C.D., The Defendant in Ecclesiastical Trials, XII-207 pp., 1942.
147. Comyns, Rev. Joseph J., C.SS.R., A.B., J.C.D., Papal and Episcopal Administration of Church Property, XIV-155 pp., 1942.
148. Barry, Rev. Garrett Francis, O.M.I., J.C.D., Violation of the Cloister, XII-260 pp., 1942.
149. Bolduc, Rev. Gatien, C.S.V., A.B., S.T.L., J.C.D., Les Études dans les Religious Cléricales, VIII-155 pp., 1942.
150. Boyle, Rev. David John, M.A., J.C.D., The Juridic Effects of Moral Certitude on Pre-Nuptial Guarantees, XII-188 pp., 1942.
151. Canavan, Rev. Walter Joseph, M.A., Litt.D., J.C.D., The Profession of Faith, XII-143 pp., 1942.
152. Desrochers, Rev. Bruno, A.B., Ph.L., S.T.B., J.C.D., Le Premier Concile Plénier de Québec et le Code de Droit Canonique, XIV-186 pp., 1942.

153. Dillon, Rev. Robert Edward, A.B., J.C.D., Common Law Marriage, X-148 pp., 1942.
154. Dodwell, Rev. Edward John, Ph.D., S.T.B., J.C.D., The Time and Place for the Celebration of Marriage, X-156 pp., 1942.
155. Donnellan, Rev. Thomas Andrew, A.B., J.C.D., The Obligation of the Missa pro Populo, VII-131 pp., 1942.
156. Eltz, Rev. Louis Anthony, A.B., J.C.D., Cooperation in Crime, XII-208 pp., 1942.
157. Gass, Rev. Sylvester Francis, M.A., J.C.D., Ecclesiastical Pensions, XI-206 pp., 1942.
158. Guiniven, Rev. John Joseph, C.SS.R., J.C.D., The Precept of Hearing Mass, XIV-188 pp., 1942.
159. Gulczynski, Rev. John Theophilus, J.C.D., The Desecration and Violation of Churches, X-126 pp., 1942.
160. Hammill, Rev. John Leo, M.A., J.C.D., The Obligations of the Traveler According to Canon 14, VIII-204 pp., 1942.
161. Haydt, Rev. John Joseph, A.B., J.C.D., Reserved Benefices, XI-148 pp., 1942.
162. Huser, Rev. Roger John, O.F.M., A.B., J.C.D., The Crime of Abortion in Canon Law, XII-187 pp., 1942.
163. Kearney, Rev. Francis Patrick, A.B., S.T.L., J.C.D., The Principles of Canon Law 1127, X-162 pp., 1942.
164. Linahen, Rev. Leo James, S.T.L., J.C.D., De Absolutione Complicis in Peccato Turpi, V-114 pp., 1942.
165. McCloskey, Rev. Joseph Aloysius, A.B., J.C.D., The Subject of Ecclesiastical Law According to Canon 12, XVII-246 pp., 1942 (printed 1943).
166. O'Neill, Rev. Francis Joseph, C.SS.R., J.C.D., The Dismissal of Religious in Temporary Vows, XIII-220 pp., 1942.
167. Prince, Rev. John Edward, A.B., S.T.B., J.C.D., The Diocesan Chancellor, X-136 pp., 1942.
168. Riesner, Rev. Albert Joseph, C.SS.R., J.C.D., Apostates and Fugitives from Religious Institutes, IX-168 pp., 1942.
169. Stenger, Rev. Joseph Bernard, J.C.D., The Mortgaging of Church Property, 186 pp., 1942.
170. Waldron, Rev. Joseph Francis, A.B., J.C.D., The Minister of Baptism, XII-197 pp., 1942.
171. Willett, Rev. Robert Albert, J.C.D., The Probative Value of Documents in Ecclesiastical Trials, X-124 pp., 1942.
172. Woeber, Rev. Edward Martin, M.A., J.C.D., The Interpellations, XII-161 pp., 1942.
173. Benko, Rev. Matthew Aloysius, O.S.B., M.A., J.C.D., The Abbot *Nullius*, XVI-148 pp., 1943.
174. Christ, Rev. Joseph James, M.A., S.T.L., J.C.D., Dispensation from Vindicative Penalties, XIV-285 pp., 1943.
175. Clancy, Rev. Patrick M. J., O.P., A.B., S.T.Lr., J.C.D., The Local Religious Superior, X-229 pp., 1943.

176. Clarke, Rev. Thomas James, J.C.D., Parish Societies, XII-147 pp., 1943.
177. Connolly, Rev. John Patrick, S.T.L., J.C.D., Synodical Examiners and Parish Priest Consultors, X-223 pp., 1943.
178. Drumm, Rev. William Martin, A.B., J.C.D., Hospital Chaplains, XII-175 pp., 1943.
179. Flanagan, Rev. Bernard Joseph, A.B., S.T.L., J.C.D., The Canonical Erection of Religious Houses, X-147 pp., 1943.
180. Kelleher, Rev. Stephen Joseph, A.B., S.T.B., J.C.D., Discussions with Non-Catholics: Canonical Legislation, X-93 pp., 1943.
181. Lewis, Rev. Gordian, C.P., J.C.D., Chapters in Religious Institutes, XII-169 pp., 1943.
182. Marx, Rev. Adolph, J.C.D., The Declaration of Nullity of Marriages Contracted Outside the Church, X-151 pp., 1943.
183. Matulenas, Rev. Raymond Anthony, O.S.B., A.B., J.C.D., Communication, a Source of Privileges, VII-225 pp., 1943.
184. O'Leary, Rev. Charles Gerard, C.SS.R., J.C.D., Religious Dismissed After Perpetual Profession, X-213 pp., 1943.
185. Power, Rev. Cornelius Michael, J.C.D., The Blessing of Cemeteries, XII-231 pp., 1943.
186. Shuhler, Rev. Ralph Vincent, O.S.A., J.C.D., Privileges of Religious to Absolve and Dispense, XII-195 pp., 1943.
187. Ziolkowski, Rev. Thaddeus Stanislaus, A.B., J.C.D., The Consecration and Blessing of Churches, XII-151 pp., 1943.
188. Heneghan, Rev. John Joseph, S.T.D., J.C.D., The Marriages of Unworthy Catholics: Canons 1065 and 1066, XVI-213 pp., 1944.
189. Carroll, Rev. Coleman Francis, M.A., S.T.L., J.C.L., Charitable Institutions.
190. Ciesluk, Rev. Joseph Edward, Ph.B., S.T.L., J.C.D., National Parishes in the United States, VI-178 pp., 1944.
191. Coburn, Rev. Vincent Paul, A.B., J.C.D., Marriages of Conscience, XII-172 pp., 1944.
192. Connors, Rev. Charles Paul, C.S.Sp., A.B., J.C.D., Extra-Judicial Procurators in the Code of Canon Law, X-94 pp., 1944.
193. Coyle, Rev. Paul Raymond, A.B., J.C.D., Judicial Exceptions, X-142 pp., 1944.
194. Fair, Rev. Bartholomew Francis, A.B., S.T.L., J.C.D., The Impediment of Abduction, XII-122 pp., 1944.
195. Gallagher, Rev. Thomas Raphael, O.P., A.B., S.T.Lr., J.C.D., The Examination of the Qualities of the Ordinand, X-166 pp., 1944.
196. Gannon, Rev. John Mark, S.T.L., J.C.D., The Interstices Required for the Promotion to Orders, XII-100 pp., 1944.
197. Goldsmith, Rev. J. William, B.C.S., S.T.L., J.C.D., The Competence of Church and State Over Marriages—Disputed Points, X-128 pp., 1944.

198. GOODWINE, REV. JOSEPH GERARD, A.B., S.T.B., J.C.D., The Reception of Converts, XIV-326 pp., 1944.
199. KOWALSKI, REV. ROMUALD EUGENE, O.F.M., A.B., J.C.D., Sustenance of Religious Houses of Regulars, X-174 pp., 1944.
200. MCCOY, REV. ALAN EDWARD, O.F.M., J.C.D., Force and Fear in Relation to Delictual Imputability and Penal Responsibility, XII-160 pp., 1944.
201. MCDEVITT, REV. VINCENT JOHN, PH.B., S.T.L., J.C.L., Perjury.
202. MARTIN, REV. THOMAS OWEN, PH.D., S.T.D., J.C.D., Adverse Possession, Prescription and Limitation of Actions: The Canonical "Praescriptio," XX-208 pp., 1944.
203. MIKLOSOVIC, REV. PAUL JOHN, A.B., J.C.L., Attempted Marriages and Their Consequent Juridic Effects.
204. MUNDY, REV. THOMAS MAURICE, A.B., S.T.L., J.C.D., The Union of Parishes, X-164 pp. 1944.
205. O'DEA, REV. JOHN COYLE, A.B., J.C.D., The Matrimonial Impediment of Nonage, VIII-126 pp., 1944.
206. OLALIA, REV. ALEXANDER AYSON, S.T.L., J.C.D., A Comparative Study of the Christian Constitution of States and the Constitution of the Philippine Commonwealth, XII-136 pp., 1944.
207. POISSON, REV. PIERRE-MARIE, C.S.C., A.B., PH.L., TH.L., J.C.L., Droits Patrimoniaux des Maisons et des Eglises Religieuses.
208. STADALNIKAS, REV. CASIMIR JOSEPH, M.I.C., J.C.D., Reservation of Censures, X-141 pp., 1944.
209. SULLIVAN, REV. EUGENE HENRY, S.T.L., J.C.D., Proof of the Reception of the Sacraments, X-165 pp., 1944.
210. VAUGHAN, REV. WILLIAM EDWARD, J.C.D., Constitutions for Diocesan Courts, X-200 pp., 1944.
211. PARO, REV. GINO, S.T.D., J.C.D., The Right of Papal Legation, X-221 pp., 1944 (printed 1947).
212. BALZER, REV. RALPH FRANCIS, C.P., J.C.D., The Computation of Time in a Canonical Novitiate, X-227 pp., 1945.
213. DOUGHERTY, REV. JOHN WHELAN, A.B., S.T.L., J.C.D., De Inquisitione Speciali, XII-195 pp., 1945.
214. DZIOB, REV. MICHAEL WALTER, J.C.D., The Sacred Congregation for the Oriental Church, XII-181 pp., 1945.
215. EIDENSCHINK, REV. JOHN ALBERT, O.S.B., B.A., J.C.D., The Election of Bishops in the Letters of Pope Gregory the Great, VIII-200 pp., 1945.
216. GILL, REV. NICHOLAS, C.P., J.C.D., The Spiritual Prefect in Clerical Religious Houses of Study, X-140 pp., 1945.
217. HYNES, REV. HARRY GERARD, S.T.L., J.C.D., The Privileges of Cardinals, XII-183 pp., 1945.
218. MCDEVITT, REV. GERALD VINCENT, S.T.L., J.C.D., The Renunciation of an Ecclesiastical Office, XIV-179 pp., 1945.

219. Manning, Rev. Joseph Leroy, J.C.D., The Free Conferral of Offices, VII-116 pp., 1945.
220. Meyer, Rev. Louis G., O.S.B., A.B., S.T.B., J.C.D., Alms-gathering by Religious, XII-163 pp., 1945.
221. O'Donnell, Rev. Cletus Francis, M.A., J.C.D., The Marriage of Minors, XII-268 pp., 1945.
222. Prunskis, Rev. Joseph, J.C.D., Comparative Law, Ecclesiastical and Civil, in Lithuanian Concordat, X-161 pp., 1945.
223. Sweeney, Rev. Francis Patrick, C.SS.R., J.C.D., The Reduction of Clerics to the Lay State, X-199 pp., 1945.
224. Vogelpohl, Rev. Henry John, J.C.D., The Simple Impediments to Holy Orders, XVI-190 pp., 1945.
225. Brockhaus, Rev. Thomas Aquinas, O.S.B., J.C.D., Religious who are known as *Conversi*, X-127 pp., 1945.
226. Griese, Rev. Orville Nicholas, S.T.D., J.C.D., The Marriage Contract and the Procreation of Offspring, XVI-224 pp., 1946.
227. Boudreaux, Rev. Warren Louis, J.C.D., The *"ab acatholicis nati"* of Canon 1099, § 2, XII-110 pp., 1946.
228. Bowe, Rev. Thomas Joseph, A.B., J.C.D., Religious Superioresses, VIII-206 pp., 1946.
229. Diederichs, Rev. Michael Ferdinand, S.C.J., J.C.D., The Jurisdiction of the Latin Ordinaries over their Oriental Subjects, XIV-153 pp., 1946.
230. Dingman, Rev. Maurice John, A.B., S.T.L., J.C.L., The Plaintiff in Contentious Trials.
231. Frison, Rev. Basil, C.M.F., M.Mus., J.C.D., The Retroactivity of Law, X-221 pp., 1946.
232. Calvin, Rev. William Anthony, M.A., J.C.D., The Administrative Transfer of Pastors, XII-288 pp., 1946.
233. Goracy, Rev. Joseph C., J.C.L., The Diriment Matrimonial Impediment of Major Orders.
234. Hale, Rev. Joseph Francis, M.A., S.T.L., J.C.D., The Pastor of Burial, X-247 pp., 1946 (printed 1949).
235. Henry, Rev. Joseph Arthur, A.B., J.C.D., The Mass and Holy Communion: Interritual Law, XII-138 pp., 1946.
236. Linenberger, Rev. Herbert, C.PP.S., J.C.D., The False Denunciation of an Innocent Confessor, VIII-205 pp., 1946 (1949).
237. Lowry, Rev. James Martin, A.B., J.C.D., Dispensation from Private Vows, XII-266 pp., 1946.
238. Lynch, Rev. George Edward, A.B., S.T.L., J.C.D., Coadjutors and Auxiliaries of Bishops, X-107 pp., 1946 (printed 1947).
239. Lynch, Rev. Timothy, M.S.SS.T., J.C.D., Contracts between Bishops and Religious Congregations, XIII-232 pp., 1946.
240. McClunn, Rev. Justin David, A.B., S.T.L., J.C.D., Administrative Recourse, VII-142 pp., 1946.

241. LOHMULLER, REV. MARTIN NICHOLAS, A.B., J.C.D., The Promulgation of Law, XII-140 pp., 1947.
242. McGRATH, REV. JAMES, A.B., J.C.D., The Privilege of the Canon, XII-156 pp., 1946.
243. MARBACH, REV. JOSEPH FRANCIS, A.B., J.C.D., Marriage Legislation for the Catholics of the Oriental Rites in the United States and Canada, XIV-314 pp., 1946.
244. SHIMKUS, REV. BERNARD ALOYSIUS, A.B., J.C.L., The Determination and Transfer of Rite.
245. SMITH, REV. VINCENT MICHAEL, A.B., S.T.L., J.C.L., Ignorance Affecting Matrimonial Consent.
246. WACHTRLE, REV. PAUL ANTHONY, A.B., J.C.L., The Baptism of the Children of Non-Catholics.
247. CROTTY, REV. MATTHEW MICHAEL, J.C.D., The Recipient of First Holy Communion, X-142 pp., 1947.
248. EAGLETON, REV. GEORGE, J.C.D., The Quinquennial Faculties, Formula IV, XIV-199 pp., 1947 (printed 1948).
249. GIBBONS, REV. MARION LEO, C.M., J.C.L., Domicile of the Wife Unlawfully Separated from Her Husband, XIV-171 pp., 1947.
250. KELLY, REV. BERNARD M., S.T.L., J.C.D., The Functions Reserved to Pastors, XII-141 pp., 1947.
251. KILCULLEN, REV. THOMAS J., LL.M., J.C.D., The Collegiate Moral Person as Party Litigant, X-150 pp., 1947.
252. LAFONTAINE, REV. GERMAINE JOSEPH, W.F., J.C.D., Relations Canoniques entre le Missionaire et Ses Superieurs, X-117 pp., 1947.
253. LANE, REV. LORAS THOMAS, A.B., S.T.L., J.C.D., Matrimonial Procedure in the Ordinary Court of Second Instance, XVI-184 pp., 1947.
254. LOVER, REV. JAMES FRANCIS, C.Ss.R., J.C.D., The Master of Novices, X-168 pp., 1947.
255. McNICHOLAS, REV. TIMOTHY JOSEPH, J.C.D., The *Septimae Manus* Witness, XII-133 pp., 1947 (printed 1949).
256. MAROSITZ, REV. JOSEPH JOHN, M.S.C., J.C.D., Obligations and Privileges of Religious Promoted to the Episcopal or Cardinalitial Dignities, XII-180 pp., 1947.
257. MURPHY, REV. FRANCIS JOSEPH, J.C.D., Legislative Powers of the Provincial Council, XII-158 pp., 1947.
258. O'BRIEN, REV. ROMAEUS WILLIAM, O.CARM., J.C.D., The Provincial Superior in Religious Orders of Men, X-294 pp., 1947.
259. PFALLER, REV. BENEDICT ANTHONY, O.S.B., J.C.D., *The ipso facto* Effected Dismissal of Religious, XII-225 pp., 1947.
260. POPEK, REV. ALPHONSE SYLVESTER, J.C.D., The Rights and Obligations of Metropolitans, XX-460 pp., 1947.
261. RISTUCCIA, REV. BERNARD JOSEPH, C.M., J.C.D., Quasi-Religious, XVI-318 pp., 1947 (printed 1949).
262. SONNTAG, REV. NATHANIEL LOUIS, O.F.M.CAP., J.C.D., Censorship of Special Classes of Books, XII-147 pp., 1947.

263. Stadler, Rev. Joseph Nicholas, J.C.D., Frequent Holy Communion, X-158 pp., 1947.
264. Szal, Rev. Ignatius Joseph, J.C.D., The Communication of Catholics with Schismatics, XII-217 pp., 1947.
265. Wagner, Rev. Urban S., O.F.M., Conv., J.C.D., Parochial Substitute Vicars and Supplying Priests, IX-126 pp., 1947.
266. Quinn, Rev. Joseph, M.A., J.C.D., Documents Required for the Reception of Orders, XIV-207 pp., 1948.
267. Bennington, Rev. James Clement, A.B., J.C.L., The Recipient of Confirmation.
268. Blaher, Rev. Damian Joseph, O.F.M., A.B., J.C.D., The Ordinary Processes in Causes of Beatification and Canonization, XVI-290 pp., 1948 (printed 1949).
269. Clune, Rev. Robert Bell, B.A., J.C.D., The Judicial Interrogation of the Parties, XII-142 pp., 1948.
270. Courtemanche, Rev. Basil F., B.A., J.C.D., The Total Simulation of Matrimonial Consent, XX-120 pp., 1948.
271. Dlouhy, Rev. Maur John, O.S.B., A.B., J.C.L., The Ordination of Exempt Religious.
272. Donovan, Rev. John Thomas, Ph.B., S.T.L., J.C.D., The Clerical Obligation of Canons 138 and 140, XII-209 pp., 1948.
273. Freking, Rev. Frederick W., A.B., S.T.B., J.C.D., The Canonical Installation of Pastors, XII-210 pp., 1948.
274. Fulton, Rev. Thomas B., J.C.D., Prenuptial Investigation, XII-190 pp., 1948.
275. Godley, Rev. James P., J.C.D., Time and Place for the Celebration of Mass, X-206 pp., 1948 (printed 1949).
276. Kane, Rev. Thomas A., A.B., B.S., J.C.D., Jurisdiction of the Patriarchs of the Major Sees in Antiquity and in the Middle Ages, XII-111 pp., 1948 (printed 1949).
277. Kennedy, Rev. Andrew A., J.C.L., The Annual Pastoral Report to the Local Ordinary.
278. Konrad, Rev. Joseph George, J.C.D., Transfer of Religious to Another Community, VIII-284 pp., 1948 (printed 1949).
279. Kress, Rev. Alphonse, J.C.L., Contumacy in Ecclesiastical Trials.
280. McCartney, Rev. Marcellus Anthony, O.F.M., M.A., J.C.D., Faculties of Regular Confessors, XII-164 pp., 1948 (printed 1949).
281. McCaslin, Rev. Edward Patrick, M.A., S.T.L., J.C.L., The Division of Parishes.
282. McElroy, Rev. Francis J., A.B., J.C.L., The Privileges of Bishops.
283. Quinn, Rev. Stephen, M.S.SS.T., J.C.D., Relation Between the Local Ordinary and Religious of Diocesan Approval, XII-153 pp., 1948 (printed 1949).
284. Schneider, Rev. Edelhard Louis, S.D.S., B.A., J.C.L., The Status of Secularized Ex-Religious Clerics, X-155 pp., 1948.

285. Thompson, Chester J., A.B., J.C.L., The Simple Removal from Office.
286. O'Brien, Rev. Kenneth R., A.B., J.C.D., The Nature of Support of Diocesan Priests in the United States, XVI-162 pp., 1949.
287. Metz, Rev. John E., S.T.L., J.C.D., The Recording Judge in the Ecclesiastical Collegiate Tribunal, X-130 pp., 1949.
288. Reinhardt, Rev. Marion J., S.T.L., J.C.D., The Rogatory Commission, XIII-182 pp., 1949.
289. Ortega Uhiuk, Rev. Juan, S.J., J.C.L., De Delicto Sollicitationis.
290. Casey, Rev. James V., J.C.D., A Study of Canon 2222 § 1, XII-127 pp., 1949.
291. Allgeier, Rev. Joseph L., J.C.D., The Canonical Obligation of Preaching in Parish Churches, X-115 pp., 1949 (printed 1950).
292. Cahill, Rev. Daniel R., J.C.D., The Custody of the Holy Eucharist, XVI-178 pp., 1949 (printed 1950).
293. Carr, Rev. Aiden, O.F.M., Carm., S.T.D., J.C.L., Vocation to the Priesthood: Its Canonical Concept.
294. Knopke, Rev. Roch F., O.F.M., J.C.D., Reverential Fear in Matrimonial Cases in Asiatic Countries: Rota Cases, XII-112 pp., 1949.
295. Lavelle, Rev. Howard D., J.C.D., The Obligation of Holding Sacred Missions in Parishes, XVI-142 pp., 1949.
296. Mickells, Rev. Anthony B., J.C.L., The Constitutive Elements of Parishes.
297. Noone, Rev. John J., J.C.D., Nullity in Judicial Acts, X-147 pp., 1949 (printed 1950).
298. Sheehan, Rev. Daniel E., J.C.L., The Minister of Holy Communion.
299. Statkus, Rev. Francis J., J.C.L., The Minister of the Last Sacraments.
300. Cook, Rev. John P., J.C.D., Ecclesiastical Communities and Their Ability to Induce Legal Customs, XII-152 pp., 1949 (printed 1950).
301. Fazzalaro, Rev. Francis J., J.C.D., The Place for the Hearing of Confessions, X-150 pp., 1949 (printed 1950).
302. Hannan, Rev. Philip M., J.C.D., The Canonical Concept of *congrua sustentatio* for the Secular Clergy, XII-237 pp., 1949 (printed 1950).
303. Quinn, Rev. Hugh G., S.T.L., J.C.L., The Particular Penal Precept.
304. Gallagher, Rev. John F., J.C.L., The Matrimonial Impediment of Public Propriety.
305. Welsh, Rev. Thomas J., J.C.L., The Use of the Portable Altar.
306. Waters, Rev. Joseph L., S.S.J., J.C.L., The Probation in Societies of Quasi-Religious.
307. Regan, Rev. Michael J., J.C.L., Canon 16.
308. Byrne, Rev. Harry J., J.C.L., Investment of Church Funds.
309. Gallagher, Rev. Thomas V., J.C.L., The Rejection of Judicial Witnesses and Testimony.
310. Chatham, Rev. Josiah G., Ph.B., S.T.L., J.C.L., Force and Fear as Invalidating Marriage: the Element of Injustice, XIV-183 pp., 1950.
311. Brown, Rev. James Victor, O.R.S.A., J.C.L., The Invalidating Effects of Force, Fear, and Fraud Upon the Canonical Novitiate.

312. Duerr, Rev. Charles J., B.A., J.C.L., The Judicial Notary.
313. Gonzalez, Rev. Francisco J., O.S.A., J.C.L., De Parocho Religioso Eiusque Superiore Locali.
314. Hannon, Rev. James J., J.C.L., Holy Viaticum.
315. Sadlowski, Rev. Erwin L., J.C.L., The Sacred Furnishings of Churches.
316. Sego, Rev. Arthur A., J.C.L., Dispensation From the Interpellations.
317. Waterhouse, Rev. John M., J.C.L., The Power of the Local Ordinary to Impose a Matrimonial Ban.
318. Frein, Rev. Eugene B., J.C.L., The Discretionary Power of the Defender of the Matrimonial Bond.
319. Carton, Rev. George A., J.C.L., The Time Factor in the Gaining of Indulgences.
320. Walsh, Rev. John J., C.S.Sp., J.C.L., The Jurisdiction of the Inter-ritual Confessor in the United States and Canada.
321. Unterkoefler, Rev. Ernest L., S.T.L., J.C.L., The Presiding Judge in Matrimonial Causes of First Instance.

www.ingramcontent.com/pod-product-compliance
Lightning Source LLC
LaVergne TN
LVHW050215080826
844660LV00012B/414

* 9 7 8 0 8 1 3 2 2 4 5 7 2 *